Delicious Drinks

Publisher's Note: Raw or semicooked eggs should not be consumed by babies, toddlers, pregnant or breast-feeding women, the elderly or those with a chronic illness.

Publisher & Creative Director: Nick Wells
Senior Project Editor: Catherine Taylor
Art Director: Mike Spender
Layout Design: Dave Jones
Digital Design & Production: Chris Herbert
Proofreader: Dawn Laker

Special thanks to Digby Smith, Helen Wall, and Gina Steer for her continued help.

This is a **FLAME TREE** Book

FLAME TREE PUBLISHING
Crabtree Hall, Crabtree Lane
Fulham, London SW6 6TY
United Kingdom
www.flametreepublishing.com

Flame Tree is part of The Foundry Creative Media Company Limited

First published 2011

11 13 15 14 12
1 3 5 7 9 10 8 6 4 2

ISBN: 978-0-85775-150-8

A copy of the CIP data for this book is available from the British Library.

Printed in China

Delicious Drinks

Quick and Easy, Proven Recipes

FLAME TREE
PUBLISHING

Contents

Just Juice 34

This chapter deals with easy-to-make juices, from drinks crammed full of delicious berries to more exotic concoctions with passion fruit, mango, and papaya. Vegetables have not been overlooked and provide a wonderful way to get children to eat their veg. Choices range from a simple carrot juice to drinks that use celery, bell peppers, and even avocado. Remember that if you use a juicer, you will get a thinner juice than if you use a blender.

Tasty Treats & Summer Smoothies 62

This chapter borders on the indulgent, featuring smoothies that are rich and creamy with the addition of ice cream, yogurt, coconut milk, chocolate, and other delicious ingredients, such as Peanut Butter Bliss. It also shows how to make smoothies packed full of juicy fruits, sodas full of luscious, cooling ice cream, and semi-frozen refreshments, such as Black Currant Granita to cool you down on a summer's day.

When feeling under the weather and run down, a detox diet can work wonders. These recipes use plenty of vegetables and fruits with herbs and extracts, all of which produce excellent results when encouraging the body to rid itself of toxins—echinacea, for example, is excellent for helping the immune system, and fresh rosemary is an excellent stimulant for circulation and the memory. This section also contains refreshing and revitalizing libations, crammed full of energy-giving foods.

There is, as the expression goes, "a time and a place," and sometimes serving an alcoholic drink is neither required nor the correct thing to do. As long as they are delicious-looking and taste divine, a nonalcoholic drink can give as much pleasure as any alcoholic one. So please all your guests, including drivers, children, mothers-to-be, and those who simply prefer to avoid alcohol, with these delicious "virgin" cocktails.

Apéritifs..174

We have adopted the word "apéritif," meaning an alcoholic drink taken before a meal in order to stimulate the appetite, from the French. Cocktails in general are often seen as apéritifs, although some, such as the classics in this section, are more appropriately drunk in this way than others. The type of liquor or liqueur served in apéritifs can be surprising—brandy is always thought of as a *digestif*, but, in fact, makes a perfect apéritif cocktail, such as in Brandy Sidecar or Brandy Classic.

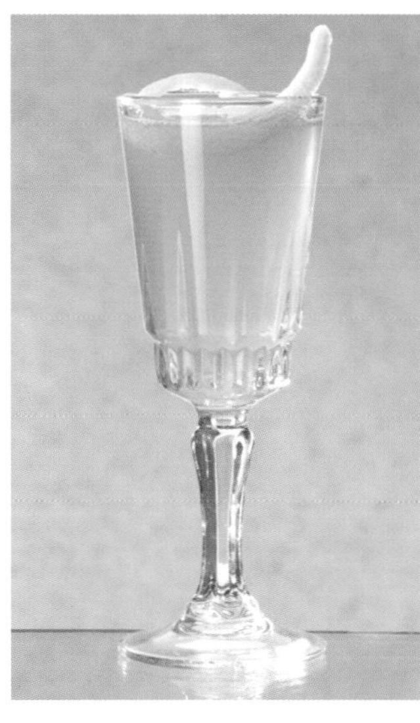

Long cocktail alternative: Tropical Bubbles, page 295

Dubonnet alternative: Napoleon, page 188

Sours & Juleps....222

Sours first appeared on the party scene in the eighteenth century and the very first was the Brandy Sour. Their sourness derives mainly from the use of a substantial amount of freshly squeezed lemon juice and lemon garnishes, with only just a minimal amount of sugar or syrup added. Created in the southern states of America, juleps are the perfect answer to long, hot, sunny days and evenings. Traditionally made from just four ingredients, nowadays there are many variations.

Sweet alternative: Egg Nog, page 304

Champagne & Sparkles 246

Champagne is the wine of celebration and its mere mention can bring a smile of pleasure and anticipation to all. It should be served with style and the rules that apply to champagne also apply to champagne cocktails. The wine should be served at around 45°F (5°F warmer than your refrigerator) in long-stemmed flutes or tulip-shape glasses that will enhance the flow of bubbles to the crown of the glass and concentrate the aroma.

Long, Short & Creamy Cocktails 282

This chapter encompasses a large range of cocktails, which include long cocktails served in tall glasses designed not only to provide a taste of alcohol but also to quench the thirst. Some have the addition of cream, giving a smooth, luxurious feel to the cocktail. Other cocktails in this section are short—with less liquid and in smaller glasses. These have a little more impact!

Cups & Punches..320

The word "punch" possibly derives from the Indian word *panch* or the Persian word *pani*, both meaning "five"—reflecting the five elements of sweet, sour, bitter, alcohol, and a weak liquid to provide the bulk. Originally, punches were made from ale, brandy, or wine. However, with the exploration of Jamaica, and the discovery of rum, punches began to increase in popularity and variation. Cups are normally not as alcoholic as punches, being made from wine and low-alcoholic liquor such as sloe gin.

Introduction

Delicious Juices and Smashing Smoothies

We all know that we need to improve our diets by eating more fruit and vegetables and, indeed, many people have taken this to heart and have already increased their intake. The World Health Organization recommends that we eat at least five portions of fruit and vegetables per day. However, for some, this is not as easy as it sounds, due to lifestyle, taste, or even economics.

Life is hectic for many people and often involves eating on the go, grabbing a bite as we rush from place to place and seldom managing to eat healthily. There is also a question of taste. We may not like some or all vegetables or even fruit. Children in particular are often fussy and picky eaters, and sometimes when they say, "I don't like this," it is easier just to take it away and not force the issue. In addition, fresh fruit and vegetables can sometimes be expensive, pushing the family budget too high.

This is where fruit juices and smoothies are the perfect answer. You can make healthy and delicious drinks, with no added extras, such as sugar, colorings, or preservatives, out of one or two fruits or vegetables for next to nothing. These will still provide a delicious drink crammed full of vitamins, minerals, and fiber. The fruits and vegetables used for juicing do not need to be uniform and perfect in size, as long as they are undamaged by bruising or are not going rotten. They will work perfectly, with an added benefit of being ready in almost no time at all—ideal for when the children come in tired and thirsty or you need a quick energy boost.

Let's not forget that juices and especially smoothies do not have to be the healthy option—they can be sweet and tasty or thick and creamy, indulgent drinks. This book contains a fabulous selection of recipes ranging from simple fruit or vegetable juices and delicious creamy smoothies, to drinks designed to lift and revitalize, others to help in healthy detoxification, and some more decadent concoctions. Adapt the recipes to suit your taste, substituting ingredients if necessary. After a couple of weeks, you will be happily juicing and smoothing at every opportunity.

Captivating Cocktails

Cocktails have enjoyed a revival over the last couple of decades, with cocktail bars opening in all major cities, either as a separate establishment or within a hotel. This has resulted in the popularity of both the classic cocktail and its exotic counterparts. Each country uses their native ingredients to produce glorious specialties that reflect their culture. However, what is a cocktail? It is a drink that can be incredibly simple, or made more complex by using two or more liqueurs or by blending liquors and mixers.

In towns and cities, cocktail bars normally open in the late afternoon to early evening, with many offering a happy hour—thus increasing their popularity enormously and introducing cocktails to a wider audience. With this boost in popularity, it is no surprise that more and more people are serving cocktails to their friends and family. Being quick and easy to make and shake, cocktails are both delicious and impressive. They can be quickly dressed up with garnishes that will wow your guests.

This book aims to simplify cocktails with a straightforward approach to their creation. There are a host of stunning recipes, from the classics, such as the Martini, to the more exotic, such as Sea Breeze, plus many other delicious drinks—both alcoholic and nonalcoholic. As well as this range of recipes, there are also hints and tips on the right glasses to use, garnishes, sweeteners, and some useful tricks of the trade; everything that would ever be required to shake, rattle, and roll.

Smoothies & Juices Equipment & Tips

Equipment and Utensils

These days, we enjoy a vast array of fruit and vegetables, ranging from home-grown varieties to tropical produce. In order to be able to prepare and make the recipes in this book, it would be useful to own certain pieces of equipment and utensils.

Juicer This is a simple machine that will extract the juice from fruits or vegetables while leaving the skin, pulp, seeds, and debris behind. All fruits and vegetables can be juiced, including parsnips, carrots, cabbage, beets, apples, pineapples, oranges, and melons. Juicers come in three types:

- **Centrifugal** All of either fruits or vegetables are fed into the machine onto a fast-spinning grater. The juice is forced through small holes in the grater, while the peel, seeds, etc. stay in the grater or are sent to a waste container that can be emptied when finished. Normally, a pitcher or cup-type container is supplied with the machine.
- **Masticating** Here, the fruits and/or vegetables are ground up into a pulp before being forced through a wire mesh with great force. These tend to be expensive, but more juice is produced than with a centrifugal machine.

• **Hydraulic** Here, the fruits and vegetables are chopped and crushed with revolving cutters. They are the most efficient of all, producing the maximum amount of juice, but they are also the most expensive.

Smoothie machine These are similar in style to a blender, having a high-sided base, where the engine is located, and a pitcher that has a nondrip pouring spout attached about one-third up from the bottom. It has tough, durable blades, designed especially for crushing ice and chopping foods. A pusher is included to ensure that everything is ground and chopped, and they have four push-control buttons. They work efficiently and quickly, producing delicious smoothies in minutes. The pitcher has useful measures so you can see at a glance how much you have made. They can be hard to clean, however, and the liquid produced tends to be very thick. It is recommended that you add 1¼ cups of liquid (water or juice) to drinks made in this way. Add it early on, along with the first ingredients, so that it sits in the bottom of the machine.

Blender This can also be called a liquidizer, and consists of a base machine and a pitcher with sturdy chopping blades. Often, the pitcher has the measurements up the sides and is ideal for softer fruits and vegetables, as well as blending juices with other ingredients. Here, the fruits and vegetables need to be prepared a little more by removing inedible parts, such as stalks, peel, seeds, and tough skins. They have speed settings, so look for one that has a good range—many now offer a pulse button, which is an excellent addition.

Lemon squeezer The simple lemon squeezer that most people have in their kitchen is vital for making juices and smoothies. It is ideal for squeezing all citrus fruits and is available in a variety of materials: glass, plastic, wood, ceramic, and aluminum.

Citrus presser This is a more powerful lemon/citrus squeezer and consists of a glass pitcher with a lemon squeezer sitting on top and a handle at the side. It is operated by simply placing half a citrus fruit on the squeezer and pulling down the handle, which operates a rod that presses out the juice into the pitcher. It is worth investing in if you plan to make a lot of juices.

Sturdy cutting board This is needed both for cutting the fruits and vegetables and for preserving your work surfaces. Keep a separate cutting board for fruits and vegetables, one for meat, and one for fish. It is important to keep all your equipment scrupulously clean, so dishwasher-safe utensils are a great investment.

Knives Good knives are essential in the preparation of all food. For these recipes, you need a cook's knife with a large, sturdy blade—essential for cutting large, tough vegetables into pieces and also for chopping herbs and fruits. You will also need a couple of other knives: a medium knife, which is ideal for cutting fruits such as melon or pineapple, plus, of course, a small vegetable knife, invaluable for preparing both fruits and vegetables.

Vegetable peeler This is also extremely useful. I prefer a swivel peeler, because it is quick and easy to use and only removes a minimal amount of peel or skin, thus helping to preserve the nutrients just under the skin.

Tips

As with many things, preparation is often key to ensuring that a good result is achieved when making smoothies and juices. Once you have the right machine and utensils, you are halfway there, but there are a few other pointers that will help you to produce delicious, nutritious drinks.

- First of all, whichever machine you have, read the instruction booklet that accompanies it. Each machine will have slightly different applications and instructions, so, for a perfect result, read the booklet first and adapt the recipe if necessary.

- Sometimes, when making a drink, it will come through too thick or even too thin—both are easy to rectify. If too thick, stir in some extra liquid or crushed ice; if too thin, pass extra fruits or vegetables through the machine and stir into the drink.

- Both fruits and vegetables are better if kept in the refrigerator before using, because this keeps them fresh and enhances their flavor. Always use plump, ripe produce.

- Frost the rim of a glass by rubbing a little citrus juice or water around the rim and dipping in superfine sugar, or even table salt for a "sour."

- Alternatively, you could add extra pieces of fruits or vegetables, cut into shapes, if liked, and wedge on the rim of the glass. Try thinly paring a long strip of citrus zest and hanging from the rim.

- Be adventurous and experiment. Once you are used to your machine, make up your own concoctions and enjoy blending different ingredients with herbs and spices.

Smoothies & Juices Ingredients

Preparation

When it comes to preparing vegetables, it is recommended to peel root vegetables, such as carrots and parsnips, but this is a personal choice and not strictly necessary.

- Cut off and discard the root if applicable as well as the leaf end and cut into chunks that will fit easily into the machine's pitcher.
- All vegetables, but green vegetables in particular, should be thoroughly washed and allowed to drain.
- Vegetables should be firm and in good condition, certainly not going rotten, with any bruised parts discarded.
- Use as fresh as possible, because the older the produce, the less of the nutrients it will contain.

The same applies to fruits.

- Use firm, sound fruits, but do ensure that they are ripe. Underripe fruits will be lacking in taste, flavor, and aroma.
- Citrus fruits are better if peeled and the bitter white pith discarded.
- Pits and seeds should be discarded and, where applicable, the fruits should be rinsed and allowed to drain.
- Fruits such as apples and pears can be left unpeeled if preferred, but do discard the core.
- Melons should be skinned and the seeds discarded.
- Pomegranates are better if the flesh and seeds are strained before using.
- Soft berries such as raspberries should be picked over and leaves or hulls discarded. Lightly rinse before using.

Beet Use either raw or cooked but not soaked in vinegar. Reputed to help kidney function. Contains folate, potassium, and magnesium.

Broccoli Use raw. High in fiber and vitamin C, beta-carotene, and antioxidants. An important food in the fight against cancer and heart disease.

Carrot Peel before using. Rich source of beta-carotene, which converts in the body to vitamin A (good for vision), plus a good antioxidant.

Celery Wash thoroughly before use. Helps to lower blood pressure.

Chile Handle with care and, when preparing, avoid touching sensitive parts of the body, such as the eyes. Wash hands thoroughly after use. Contains antioxidants, is good for stimulating the metabolic rate and helps to lower blood cholesterol levels. Also contains high levels of capsaicin, a natural painkiller.

Cucumber Part of the squash family. Comes in two varieties, smaller ones for pickles, and the more common English, or hothouse, large cucumber sold in the stores. Can act as a mild diuretic and photochemical that can help reduce cholesterol levels in the blood.

Fennel Wash thoroughly, discarding the root. Leafy tops can be used as garnish. Contains small amounts of beta-carotene and potassium.

Okra Also called Lady's Fingers. Trim off the tops before using and use within 1–2 days of purchase. Contains seeds inside the vegetable, which are used as a thickener in Creole dishes. Very good source of soluble fiber, good for lowering cholesterol levels.

Parsnip Peel and discard top before use and cut into chunks. Flesh has a sweet flavor. Contains a moderate amount of fiber, beta-carotene, vitamin B_1 and niacin, essential with the other B vitamins for growth and a healthy nervous system.

Peppers, bell: green, red, and yellow Green bell peppers are one of the best vegetable sources of vitamin C. All bell peppers are high in beta-carotene as well as rich in vitamin C. As with chiles, all are high in capsaicin, a natural painkiller, and reputed to be helpful in alleviating the pain from arthritis.

Sweet potato Peel before use. Normally an orange-fleshed tuber, rich in beta-carotene (the white-fleshed sweet potato is not). Both varieties contain good quantities of vitamins C and E and are a great source of slow-release carbohydrates.

Tomato Technically a fruit, tomatoes come in many different shapes, sizes, and colors. A rich source of lycopene, an important antioxidant in the prevention of heart disease and cancer. Also contains beta-carotene and vitamins C and E.

Zucchini Trim and peel before use. Member of the squash family. Low in calories and a good smoothie base due to high water content.

Fruits

Apple Eaters and cookers, normally kept for cooking, come in many varieties. Choose firm, unblemished fruits with plenty of juice. Contains vitamin C. No need to peel but core first.

Apricot Small, orange-colored fruit with a slightly hairy, edible skin and pit which needs removing. High in beta-carotene. Very sweet, especially when dried.

Banana Skin is green when underripe and turns yellow on ripening. Rich in vitamins B_6 and C. Popular food because easily eaten and digested. Peel before using.

Blackberry Grown both wild and cultivated and contains significant amounts of vitamin E, flavonoids, and ellagic acid, which helps to block cancer cells. Rinse lightly before using.

Black currant Rich source of vitamin C and the anti-cancer carotenoid lutein. Grown for commercial preparations instead of being sold as fruit. Strip from the stalks, rinse, and use.

Blueberry Small blue/black berries. Rinse before using. Highly nutritious and good in the fight against cancer, especially when dried.

Coconut Large fruit with a hard, hairy outer casing or husk. To remove from the outer casing, smash with a mallet to reveal the inner fruit. Pierce this carefully to drain off the coconut milk first. Coconut is high in saturated fat, although many believe that this fat is not as harmful as animal or dairy saturated fats.

Fig Grown extensively in hot climates, coming in red, green, and purple varieties. Can be eaten fresh or dried. Wash fresh figs before using. Contains small amounts of carbohydrate and beta-carotene.

Grapefruit Three varieties are available: pink, red, and yellow, with yellow being the most common and also more tart than the other two. Contains good amounts of vitamin C. Peel and discard the bitter white pith before using.

Grape Comes in three colors: green, red, and black, both seedless and seeded. Red grapes contain polyphenols, also found in red wine, which help in the fight against heart disease, and some research shows it can help against cancer.

Kiwi Grown extensively in New Zealand and now available in both green and gold varieties. Small fruit with a brown, slightly hairy skin, the flesh containing tiny edible black seeds. Peel before using. A rich source of vitamin C.

Mango Grown extensively in India as well as the Caribbean and other tropical countries. A green/yellow smooth skin with bright orange flesh around a large pit. Peel, cut off the flesh, and use raw. Very rich in fiber, especially soluble fiber. Helps to keep cholesterol low and also contains vitamin E and antioxidants. Let rest until ripe before using.

Melon Divided into two classes, either muskmelon or watermelon, several varieties are readily available. Muskmelons include honeydew, with bright yellow skin and pale flesh, cantaloupe, casaba, and crenshaw.

Orange Rich in vitamin C and flavonoids, which have a good antioxidant effect on the body. Peel and discard the bitter white pith before using.

Papaya Also called pawpaw. An elongated fruit with a green skin that turns yellow as it ripens. Rich in beta-carotene and an excellent source of soluble fiber.

Passion fruit Small, dark purple fruit that wrinkles once ripe. Both the flesh and seeds are edible. Contains vitamin C.

Peach/nectarine Both members of the same family. Flesh is normally yellow but a white flesh variety is occasionally available during the summer months. Contain vitamin C and a trace of soluble fiber.

Pear Many varieties are available, including Bartlett, Bosc, and Comice. Normally picked underripe and allowed to ripen slowly. Contains vitamin C and potassium.

Pineapple Grown in most tropical and subtropical countries. The attractive plume needs discarding before eating, as do the skin and hard central core. Contains bromelain, which breaks down protein, making it easier to digest.

Plum Many different varieties are available, including damsons and greengages. All are excellent sources of fiber, with the red-skinned varieties containing beta-carotene.

A History of Cocktails

The golden age of the cocktail got into full swing during the 1920s and 1930s. After Prohibition ended in 1933, barmen were free to show off and develop their mixing flare in making the drinks that had originally become popular as a way of masking the not-so-fine taste of the bootlegged liquor of the era.

However, "cocktails" were invented much earlier than the 1920s, it seems, with the first recorded uses of the term appearing in the first decade of the nineteenth century. One publication of Hudson, New York—*The Balance and Columbian Repository*—stated in May 1806 that the "Cocktail is a stimulating liquor composed of spirits of any kind, sugar, water, and bitters ..."

Etymological Mystery

On the subject of how this kind of drink came to be called a "cocktail," however, there is little consensus and many stories, some of which indicate that the origin stretches back into the eighteenth century. Many of the most obvious etymological tales relate to the cockerel's tail feather in some way. One tells how, during the American Revolution, a certain tavern landlady named Betsy Flanagan served up stolen chicken to the soldiers and then used the tail feathers to decorate her popular mixed drinks, eliciting cries of admiration for the liquor and beautiful cocks' tails, to which one French soldier supposedly cried, "Vive le cocktail!" Alternatively, it has been said that officers, who perhaps frequented Betsy's tavern, made a toast with such a drink to the feathers in George Washington's hat.

It has also been suggested that "cocktail" is a mutation of "cock ale," which was both a beer using an old cockerel as an ingredient, and a concoction of bread and alcohol that was fed to cockerels to improve their performance in cockfights and drunk by the human participants in victory celebration.

Another colonial tavern theory is that, when liquors started to run low in the barrel and thus lost some of their taste and quality, they were run together into one barrel and these "tailings" of alcohol were served as a lower-priced mixed drink from the "cock" stop. Finally, a different hypothesis altogether suggests that the term, in fact, derives from the mispronunciation of the French word *coquetier*, which was an egg-cuplike vessel in which such drinks were served or mixed.

Early Cocktails

One of the first cocktails ever invented appears to be the Sazerac, as named by John Schiller in 1859 after his newly opened Sazerac Coffee House in New Orleans, Louisiana. It was based on a combination of cognac and proprietary bitters mixed by Antoine Amédée Peychaud—apparently in a *coquetier*; but it would come to exist in many forms using a range of different ingredients. Commonly used measures are 2 parts brandy or rye whiskey, 1 dash Peychaud's bitters, 1 teaspoon sugar or sugar syrup, and 1 teaspoon absinthe (or pastis, which is more easily obtained) to coat the glass. We have provided a recipe for a Vodka Sazerac on page 239.

Whether defined by the purists as a short drink consisting of alcohol and juice or mixers, or in the widest sense any kind of mixed drink containing spirits, hundreds of cocktails have been invented over the years. Ranging from early classics such as the Martini and the Margarita (often with their own stories as to how they came about), to Piña Colada and Sex on the Beach – whatever your tastes, there is a cocktail out there for everyone.

Cocktail Equipment

By no means do you need a vast artillery of tools, gadgets, and ingredients to make a good cocktail, but there are some things that are essential and others that will make life a whole lot easier or add that extra sparkle to your experience. This section will prove invaluable, so make sure you read it in advance of heading to the store, so you can feel confident that all the bases are covered.

Corkscrew There are many on the market and it really is a question of personal preference. I would recommend buying a cheap corkscrew with a spiral cone, because these tend to last for ever.

Cocktail Shaker Has two essential uses: combines the ingredients quickly and easily, as well as chilling the drink when shaken with ice. Two types include:

- **Standard Cocktail Shaker or Cobbler Shaker** Normally made of three pieces: a metal (usually stainless steel) outside casing, a lid, and a tight-fitting cap. There is usually a built-in strainer and the inside is often made of glass. Some have a tap on the side for cocktails that do not need straining.

- **Boston Shaker** Similar to a standard shaker and looks like the shakers used by professional bartenders. Has no strainer and consists of two parts.

Mixing Glass Used for stirring drinks, not shaking. Rolling a cocktail refers to rolling the cocktail from one mixing glass to another.

Spoons Long- or short-handle spoons are ideal to use as stirrers.

Blender These are useful for crushing ice. You will not need a large blender—simply one small enough to sit on or under the bar.

Ice Tongs For handling ice cubes—again, a case of personal preference.

Juice Extractor and Strainer Again, there are many juice extractors and strainers on the market, from a simple lemon squeezer with a small strainer over a glass pitcher to a smoothie machine with an outlet tap.

Pitcher There are two types of pitcher:

• **The Metal Cocktail Pitcher** More common before the 1930s, this pitcher had a spout and lid and looked like a coffeepot.

• **The Glass Martini Pitcher** Popular in the 1940s and 1950s, this pitcher is a tall glass pitcher with a stirrer.

Cloths For polishing glasses before using.

Decorating

There is a plethora of accessories to add that something extra to your cocktail:

Toothpicks Ideal for garnishes, both the normal short sticks or wooden kebab sticks cut down to about 4 inches threaded with fruits and balanced across the glass.

Knives A small sharp knife to use to cut fruit. A canella knife to remove thicker strands of citrus peel and to make spirals for garnishing.

Zester Good for making long thin shreds of citrus peel for use as a garnish.

Other Decorations From umbrellas and fancy stirrers with a motif or an amusing animal, to flowers or vegetables, the choice again is personal.

Straws Ideal for long drinks—bendable or straight.

Cocktail Measures & Glasses

Measures

Knowing what the different measures are is vital to be able to mix a successful cocktail. Obviously, you will need a measuring cup or pitcher as well as the measure cap that is on top of the cocktail shaker. Shot glasses vary, so the cocktail recipes in this book use measures for most alcohol ingredients.

1 measure = 1 fl. oz. = 1 tbsp. plus 2 tsp.
2 measures = 1¾ fl. oz. = 3 tbsp. plus 1 tsp.
3 measures = 2⅔ fl. oz. = 5 tbsp.
4 measures = 3⅓ fl oz = ¼ cup plus 3 tbsp.
1 bottle liquor = 24 fl. oz. = 3 cups
1 bottle wine = 25½ fl. oz. = scant 3¼ cups

Types of Glasses

All glasses should be absolutely spotless and, even if washed in a dishwasher, it is always a good idea to polish the glasses with a clean, dry dish towel before use. Before starting, check how many measures your glasses hold, then keep each size together.

Classic Cocktail Glass
Triangular shape (or V-shape) with a long stem. Holds about 5 fl. oz.

Double Cocktail Glass
A short glass with a saucer cup on a short stem. Holds about 8 fl. oz.

Hurricane or Piña Colada Glass A bulbous, tall glass on a medium high stem. Holds 14 fl. oz.

Margarita Glass
A straight-sided glass with a small bowl at the top of a tall stem, with a wide saucer at the top of the glass. This gives a wide rim, which is perfect for the salt effect for serving margaritas. Usually holds about 7 fl. oz.

Coupe Glass A short glass on a stem, about 6 inches high with a wide-necked bowl around 4 inches wide.

Old-Fashioned Glass A stubby glass with a thick bottom, cut glass or clear. Holds about 8 fl. oz. It was the original glass for a cocktail and is now most often used for all shorts, such as gin and tonic.

Highball Glass A tall glass, normally clear. Holds 10 fl. oz.

Collins Glass A tall, clear glass. Holds 12 fl. oz.

Fluted Champagne Glass A tulip-shaped glass on a tall stem. Holds 5 fl. oz.

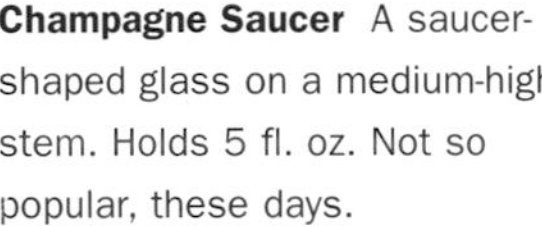

Champagne Saucer A saucer-shaped glass on a medium-high stem. Holds 5 fl. oz. Not so popular, these days.

Wine Glass A wide variety available—red wine glasses are larger than white, with a large bowl (for the nose) on a tall stem. They can be either crystal or plain glass and normally hold about 7 fl. oz., but it varies.

Punch Glass Punch glasses are generally sturdy enough to withstand hot liquids and often either have a handle or sit in a metal holder. Because they are normally shaped like short glasses, it is easy to eat the fruit that is often put in punches.

Cocktail Ingredients & Tips

Liqueurs Liqueurs, such as crème de cacao, crème de menthe, and curaçao, come in a variety of colors, but there is no noticeable difference in taste. While the recipes may specify the use of a certain color, it is not necessary to strictly adhere to this recommendation; feel free to experiment with different shades.

Cream of Coconut Look for cans of cream of coconut that are sweetened (not to be confused with the unsweetened varieties for culinary purposes in ethnic grocery stores). Cream of coconut is available at both grocery stores and liquor stores.

Table Salt This is ideal for **frosting** the rims of cocktails, especially sours—simply place a small amount in a saucer as wide as the glass. Dip the glass in water, egg white, or lemon juice, shake off the excess, and place in the salt. Press down until well coated, then let dry before using.

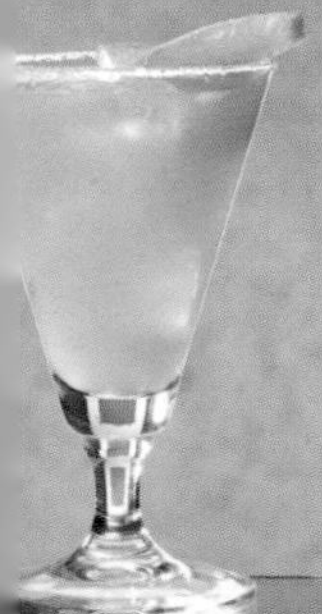

Sugar Use superfine sugar as above in place of salt for drinks that are sweeter. If you do not have superfine sugar, process regular granulated sugar in a blender for 1 minute, thereby reducing it to a finer size. Confectioners' sugar, or powdered sugar, is sometimes also used.

Sugar Syrup Many recipes call for some sweetness. This can be either honey or sugar syrup. I would recommend making the syrup in small amounts and using it freshly made. After a long period, the syrup could start to crystallize. Make sugar syrup as follows: use heaping 1 cup white granulated sugar and ⅔ cup water; place the sugar and water in a heavy saucepan and place over a gentle heat; heat gently, stirring occasionally, until the sugar has completely dissolved; bring to a boil and boil steadily (to a temperature of 221°F) until a light syrup is formed; remove from the heat. Let stand to cool, then pour into a screw-top sterilized bottle. When cold, screw down the lid. Use as required.

Chocolate This can be grated and used to frost glasses (using egg white) in the same way as salt and sugar.

Eggs Eggs are used in order to make a drink sparkling clear; they do not affect the taste of the drink, so can be left out if preferred. Make sure that the eggs used are as fresh as possible. A good test for this is to place a raw egg in its shell in a bowl of water; if it sinks to the bottom, it is fresh; but if it floats to the surface, it is stale.

Milk and Cream Again, make sure the milk or cream is very fresh, of the best quality available, and use chilled.

Fruit Use fruits that are ripe and unblemished; do not use any sections that are bruised.

Ice

- The quality of the ice used in cocktails is of paramount importance. Water with a strong fluoride flavor or from a hard-water area will affect the taste of the drink. Ice is used in many cocktails to cleanse and give a crystal clear appearance, so use filtered or bottled noncarbonated water, or use purification tablets to clean the water.
- Make ice on a regular basis; do not be tempted to make a large amount to keep in the freezer.
- Always use crushed ice immediately because it will quickly dissolve.
- Crushed ice can be made in a blender, but you will need to check that your machine has metal instead of plastic blades. Before placing in the blender, break the ice cubes down a little as follows (otherwise,

trying to crush them could seriously overload the blender motor): place the ice in a heavy-duty plastic bag and then in a clean dish towel; smash with a rolling pin or meat mallet, or even a clean hammer will do; then place in the blender and process until crushed, using the pulse button.

- In order to make broken ice, simply follow the plastic bag stage for the making of crushed ice.
- When the recipe uses the crushed ice with the other ingredients in a cocktail shaker, this is to produce a clear drink. Straining the cocktail from the shaker removes any unwanted particles (such as with citrus fruit juice) and any remaining crushed ice.
- When shaking a drink that contains egg or cream, it is nearly always done with crushed ice in the cocktail shaker. The aim is to freeze the drink halfway while at the same time breaking down and blending the different ingredients.

More Cocktail Hints and Tips

There are a few guidelines that will significantly help make the mixing of cocktails easier:

- Keep all the ingredients to be used as cool as possible and, where applicable, such as with fruit juices, keep them in the refrigerator. When the weather is particularly hot, chill the glasses first.
- Make sure that the work surface is clean and will not be ruined if some alcohol is spilled on it.

- Have a large pitcher of warm water nearby for rinsing purposes.
- When serving warm or hot punches or cups, use heatproof glasses with stay-cool handles and warm the glasses before filling.
- Never try out a new cocktail on guests—try it yourself first, because it may need some adjustments.
- Do not waste malt whiskey in a cocktail—these whiskies are designed to be drunk without mixers.
- Do not shake a drink that has a carbonated liquid in it.
- After shaking a cocktail that either has a very distinctive flavor or contains cream, always wash out the shaker before reusing.

Just Juice

Ugli Juice

SERVES 1

Ingredients

1 ugli fruit
1 wedge ripe honeydew melon
few black seedless grapes
chilled sparkling water, to dilute (optional)
extra grapes and mint sprig, to decorate (optional)

Method

Peel the ugli fruit, discarding the peel and pith. Cut the flesh into chunks. Remove any seeds from the melon and discard the skin. Cut into chunks. Remove the grapes from their stalks and rinse lightly. Add to the ugli along with the melon. Pass through a juicer or blender until the juice is formed. Pour into the glass and dilute with water, if using. Decorate the glass with a mint sprig and a few grapes, if using, by hanging little bunches over the rim of the glass.

Ugli fruits are similar to grapefruit and are, in fact, a cross between a grapefruit and a tangerine. They are sweeter in taste than the yellow grapefruit, similar to the pink variety. They are difficult to find, so snap them up when in season.

ALTERNATIVE Use either pink or red grapefruit if ugli fruit is not available and, if preferred, strain through a fine strainer to produce a smooth juice.

Apple & Raspberry Juice

SERVES 1

Ingredients

2 apples, such as Golden Delicious
1¾ cups fresh or thawed frozen raspberries
⅔ cup orange juice
ice cubes, to serve
chilled sparkling water, to dilute (optional)
mint sprig, to decorate

Method

Cut the apples into quarters and discard the cores. Chop into chunks. Pass through a juicer or blender with the raspberries and orange juice (if using a blender) until the juice is formed. Stir in the orange juice if not already used, then pour over ice cubes in glasses and dilute with sparkling water, if using. Float a mint sprig on top and serve.

This juice can be made using either fresh or thawed frozen raspberries. If using thawed frozen raspberries, you may find that it produces a little more juice than fresh.

ALTERNATIVE Add a mixture of berries to the apples—try blackberries, strawberries, or blueberries.

Berry Juice

SERVES 1

Berries, such as strawberries, blueberries, blackberries, and raspberries, are available all year round, so there is no need to keep this delicious juice just for the summer months. Strawberries are an excellent source of vitamin C, while raspberries and blackberries are high in fiber and blueberries are reputed to have anti-carcinogenic qualities.

Ingredients

6 oz. ripe strawberries
1 cup ripe raspberries
⅓ cup ripe blackberries
ice cubes, to serve
chilled mineral water, to dilute (optional)
mint sprig and extra berries, to decorate

Method

Hull the strawberries, rinse, and cut in half. Lightly rinse the raspberries and blackberries. Pass through a juicer or blender until the juice is formed. Place the ice cubes into a glass, pour over the juice, dilute to taste with the water, if using, decorate, and serve immediately.

ALTERNATIVE Use each fruit separately to make a single flavored juice. Dilute with iced water, if liked, in place of the ice cubes. If left for a little while, the juices may need stirring before drinking.

Melon Trio

SERVES 2

Ingredients

1 wedge ripe honeydew melon
1 wedge ripe cantaloupe melon
1 wedge ripe galia melon
small piece ginger, peeled and grated
chilled mineral water, to dilute (optional)
ice cubes, to serve
mint sprigs, to decorate

Method

Discard any seeds from the melon wedges and cut off the skin. Cut the flesh into chunks and pass through a juicer or blender together with the ginger until the juice is formed. Pour into tall glasses, dilute with mineral water, if using, and add ice cubes. Drape mint sprigs over the side and serve immediately.

These days, we can buy a good variety of melons throughout the year. These include the red-flesh watermelon, orange-flesh charentais, light green honeydew, the similarly pale green to golden galia, and the fragrant orange-flesh cantaloupe. Vary the juice according to availability and taste.

ALTERNATIVE Add 2–3 peeled and seeded clementines to the melons prior to juicing and use a few segments to decorate the glasses.

Melon with Passion Fruit Juice

SERVES 1

Passion fruits are at their best when they are at their ugliest. They need to be very wrinkled—if smooth, the fruit will be underripe and the wonderful aromatic flavor will not be at its best.

Ingredients

2 wedges honeydew melon
1 wedge galia melon
2 ripe passion fruits
chilled sparkling water, to dilute (optional)
ice cubes, to serve

Method

Discard any seeds from the melon wedges and remove the skin. Cut the flesh into chunks. Scoop out the flesh and seeds from one and a half of the passion fruits and add to the melon flesh. Pass through a juicer or blender until the juice is formed. Pour into the glass. Add sparkling water to dilute, if using, and add the ice cubes. Scoop out the seeds from the remaining half of the passion fruit and spoon on top of the juices. Serve immediately.

ALTERNATIVE Use the flesh and seeds of 3 passion fruits in the juice and top the glasses of juice with a teaspoonful of finely chopped melon flesh.

Mango & Orange Juice

SERVES 1

Mangoes provide an excellent source of antioxidant carotenoids and are extremely rich in soluble fiber and a good source of vitamin E. Buy mangoes a few days before they are required, because they are best eaten completely ripe.

Ingredients

2 large, ripe mangoes
2 large oranges
chilled sparkling water, to dilute (optional)
ice cubes, to serve
thinly pared orange zest and mint sprig, to decorate

Method

Peel the mangoes and cut the flesh away from the large pit. Cut the flesh into chunks. Using a vegetable peeler, carefully pare off two long thin strips of orange zest and reserve. Peel the remaining zest and bitter white pith off both oranges and divide into segments. Discard the seeds and add to the mangoes. Pass through a juicer or blender until the juice is formed. Pour into the glass, dilute with water, if using, and add the ice cubes. Drape the orange zest down the sides of the glass, add the mint sprig, and serve.

ALTERNATIVE Canned mangoes can be used if ripe ones are not available. Drain before using. Ripe papayas can also be used, but discard the skin and black seeds before juicing.

Tropical Fruit Juice

SERVES 2

Ingredients

1 ripe mango
1 papaya
1 ripe passion fruit
½ medium, ripe pineapple
chilled mineral water, to dilute (optional)
ice cubes, to serve
mint sprigs, to decorate

It is important to ensure that the fruits to be juiced are at their best and perfectly ripe. If beginning to bruise, the fruits may be overripe and the flavor will not be as good.

Method

Peel the mango and cut the flesh away from the pit. Discard the peel and seeds from the papaya and cut into chunks. Add to the mango. Scoop the flesh and seeds from the passion fruit and, if liked, strain to remove the seeds. Add to the other fruit. Remove the plume and skin from the pineapple and cut lengthwise into four. Discard the hard central core from the pineapple and cut into chunks. Reserve 2–4 pieces of pineapple and add the remainder to the mango, passion fruit, and papaya. Pass through a juicer or blender until the juice is formed. Pour into glasses and dilute with water, if using. Add the ice cubes and decorate the glasses with the reserved pineapple and mint sprigs. Serve.

ALTERNATIVE For a thicker, creamier juice, add 1 large, ripe, peeled banana before juicing.

Pear & Raspberry Juice

SERVES 1

Ingredients

2 ripe pears, such as Bosc or Comice
1 medium orange
1 cup fresh or thawed frozen raspberries
chilled mineral water, to dilute (optional)
ice cubes, to serve
mint sprig, to decorate
1 tsp. grated chocolate (optional)

Method

Peel and core the pears, then peel the orange, discarding the bitter white pith, and divide into segments. Lightly rinse the raspberries, if using fresh, and reserve a few for decoration; add to the pears. Pass through a juicer or blender until the juice is formed. Pour into the glass, dilute with water, if using, add the ice cubes, then decorate. If feeling indulgent, sprinkle the top with grated chocolate.

As with all fruits, it is important when eating pears that they are ripe. Otherwise, pears especially lack taste and their texture is woody. Which variety you choose is often a question of taste and familiarity. Unlike many fruits, pears are not normally sold ripe but need to ripen at home. This can take as long as one week but is well worth the wait.

ALTERNATIVE Omit the raspberries and add the flesh and seeds of 3 ripe passion fruits. Process until blended, then pass through a fine strainer to remove the seeds.

Red Grape Juice with Apple

SERVES 1

Ingredients

1 cup red seedless grapes
2 green apples
2 tbsp. orange juice
chilled sparkling water,
  to dilute (optional)
ice cubes, to serve
mint sprig, to decorate

Method

Remove the grapes from their stalks and rinse lightly; reserve a few for decoration. Cut the apples into quarters and discard the cores. Rinse if not peeling, then cut into chunks. Add to the grapes together with the orange juice and pass through a juicer or blender until the juice is formed. Pour into the glass and dilute with the water, if using. Add the ice cubes, decorate, and serve.

Juice made from red grapes contains the same properties as red wine: polyphenols, an antioxidant and a powerful aid against heart disease, and ellagic acid, which has cancer-fighting properties. Both excellent reasons to make this one of your favorites!

ALTERNATIVE Use this juice as the basis for a nonalcoholic Pimm's. Pour half the amount of juice into a pitcher and add some ice cubes. Add pieces of chopped fruits, such as apples, pears, strawberries, peaches, and cucumber, and top off with lemon-flavored soda. Float some washed mint sprigs on top. Let stand for 5 minutes, then stir and serve.

Guava & Mango Juice

SERVES 1

Ingredients

4 ripe guavas
1 large ripe mango
1–2 tsp. honey (optional)
chilled mineral water, to dilute (optional)
lemon or lime slices, to decorate

Method

Peel the guavas, discard the seeds, and chop into chunks. Peel the mango and cut the flesh away from the pit. Chop and add to the guavas. Pass through a juicer or blender until the juice is formed. Taste and, if liked, add a little honey. Pour into a tall glass and dilute with water, if using, stir, decorate, and serve.

Guavas can be bought fresh or canned, but wherever possible use fresh. If using canned, drain well before use. Guavas should be used ripe, so look for fruits that have a light yellow skin and yield when pressed lightly with the fingers.

ALTERNATIVE Replace the mango with 1 large, ripe, peeled, seeded papaya and in place of the iced water, place ice cubes in the glass and pour the juice over before serving.

Orange & Pomegranate Juice

SERVES 2

Ingredients

3 large oranges
2 pomegranates
ice cubes, to serve
chilled mineral water, to dilute (optional)

Method

Peel the oranges, discarding the bitter white pith, and cut the flesh into chunks. Cut the pomegranates in half and scoop out all the seeds. Reserve a few seeds, if liked, for decoration. Place the seeds with the oranges and pass through a juicer or blender until juiced. Place some ice cubes in the glasses and pour over the juice. Dilute with water, if using. Scatter with the reserved pomegranate seeds, if using, and serve.

Pomegranates are one of the few fruits that are not available all year round, so take advantage of them when in season—normally around Christmas time.

ALTERNATIVE Replace the oranges with 2 wedges honeydew melon. Remove the seeds and skin, chop into small chunks, and blend with the pomegranate.

Persimmon & Peach Juice

SERVES 1

Persimmons are not the best fruits to eat raw if they are not ripe. However, once ripe, they are very sweet and juicy and it is well worth waiting for the fruits to ripen.

Ingredients

3 ripe persimmons
2 ripe peaches or nectarines
chilled mineral water, to serve
strawberry slices and blackcurrants, to decorate

Method

Discard the stalks from the persimmons, rinse lightly, and chop. Lightly rinse the peaches or nectarines, cut in half, discard the pits, and cut into chunks. Add to the persimmons and pass through a juicer or blender until the juice is formed. Dilute with the water and pour into a glass. Decorate and serve immediately.

ALTERNATIVE Replace the iced water with ⅔ cup orange juice.

Apple & Blackberry Juice

SERVES 1

Apples and blackberries must be one of the most popular combinations of fruits, but they are rarely used for juices. Look for large, plump blackberries that are bursting with flavor and juice.

Ingredients

2 large apples
1½ cups ripe blackberries
1–2 tsp. honey (optional)
ice cubes, to serve
chilled sparkling water, to dilute (optional)
2 mint sprigs

Method

Lightly rinse the apples and blackberries. Cut the apples into quarters, discard the core, cut into chunks, and add to the blackberries. Pass through a juicer or blender until the juice is formed. Taste and add the honey, if liked. Place the ice cubes in the glass, pour over the juice, dilute with water, if using, decorate with mint sprigs, and serve.

ALTERNATIVE Replace the blackberries with the same amount of ripe black currants. You may need to increase the amount of honey, depending on how ripe the black currants are.

Watermelon with Ginger

SERVES 1

Ingredients

1 large wedge watermelon
small piece fresh ginger
1 lemongrass stalk
ice cubes, to serve

Method

Discard the skin and seeds from the watermelon and cut into chunks. Peel the ginger, chop, and add to the melon. Discard the outer leaves from the lemongrass, chop, and add to the melon. Pass through a juicer or blender until the juice is formed. Place ice cubes into a tall glass, pour in the juice, and serve.

When using ginger with juices, it is recommended that you use fresh ginger instead of ground, because a far better flavor is achieved. Use a small, sharp knife to peel the ginger and cut into small chunks.

ALTERNATIVE Add the juice and flesh from 2 limes in place of the lemongrass stalk. If a sweeter juice is preferred, add a little honey.

Carrot & Orange Juice

SERVES 2

Ingredients

3 large carrots
2 large oranges
3–4 tbsp. mineral water, to blend (optional)
chilled mineral water, to dilute
orange slices and Italian parsley, to decorate

Method

Peel the carrots and chop into chunks. Peel and discard the bitter white pith from the oranges and divide into segments. Pass the carrots and orange segments through a juicer or blender until the juice is formed. If using a blender, add 3–4 tablespoons water when blending. Pour into tall glasses, diluting with water, if using, decorate, and serve.

Carrots and oranges are a popular blend of flavors and offer a very healthy choice. The resulting juice is full of vitamin C from the oranges as well as flavonoids, which have antioxidant properties. Carrots are also a rich source of beta-carotene as well as vitamin A.

ALTERNATIVE Increase the number of carrots to 6 large and omit the oranges. Use ⅔ cup chilled mineral water if using a blender. Using large carrots is faster than using smaller carrots.

Carrot, Beet & Apple

SERVES 1

You can, if you prefer, use cooked beet in this juice—it is easier and quicker to use than raw and will yield slightly more juice.

Ingredients

3 large carrots
4 oz. beet (see note above)
2 Granny Smith apples
1 celery stalk or ½ tsp. celery salt (or to taste)
chilled mineral water, to dilute (optional)
ice cubes, to serve (optional)
celery stalk, for stirring

Method

Peel the carrots and cut into chunks. Peel the beet, discarding the root and stalks, and cut into chunks. Cut the apples into quarters, discard the cores, and chop coarsely. Add to the carrot and beet, along with the trimmed, washed, and chopped celery stalk, if using. Pass through a juicer or blender until the juice is formed, adding celery salt to taste, if liked. Pour into the glass, dilute with the water, if using, add ice cubes, and serve with a celery stalk for stirring.

ALTERNATIVE Omit the apple and celery salt and replace with 3 celery stalks that have been trimmed, washed, and chopped.

Tomato Juice

SERVES 2

Ingredients

1 lb. ripe tomatoes
pinch sugar
chilled mineral water, to dilute (optional)
ice cubes, to serve
lemon slices, cherry tomatoes, and basil leaves, to decorate (optional)
few dashes Worcestershire sauce (optional)

Method

Lightly rinse the tomatoes and chop coarsely. Pass through a juicer or blender until the juice is formed, then add sugar to taste and dilute with water, if using. Place a few ice cubes in tall glasses and pour over the tomato juice. Decorate as liked, add the Worcestershire sauce, if using, and serve.

Tomato Juice must be the best-known and popular of all 'vegetable' juices. Apart from being a staple juice that can be used in many different ways, it can also have many different vegetables added to it, giving a vast array of flavors that will suit most tastes. Try doing a little experimenting of your own—by adding chile, garlic, herbs, curry-style spices, vegetables, or even some fruits.

ALTERNATIVE Add a little Tabasco sauce in place of the Worcestershire sauce, along with some fresh basil leaves and 2–4 garlic cloves; or try a selection of fresh herbs: thyme, parsley, rosemary, or cilantro.

Cucumber & Apple Juice

SERVES 1

Ingredients

1 English cucumber
freshly ground sea salt, to sprinkle (optional)
2 Granny Smith apples
2 tbsp. orange juice
chilled mineral water, to dilute (optional)
few fresh mint sprigs

As a member of the squash family, cucumber is naturally a juicy vegetable. When sprinkled lightly with a little freshly ground salt, a cucumber will become even juicier. If you have smaller ridged cucumbers normally used for pickling, you can substitute two of them for the English cucumber. Both will work well here.

Method

Cut off and reserve a few thin slices of cucumber. Peel the remainder, then cut into thick slices, place in a colander, and add a twist or two of freshly ground sea salt, if using. Let stand for 5–10 minutes. Quarter the apples and discard the cores, then chop. Pass all the ingredients through a juicer or blender until the juice is formed. Pour the juice into the glass, dilute with water, if using, and decorate with the reserved cucumber slices and mint sprigs.

ALTERNATIVE Simply place the peeled, chopped cucumber into a smoothie machine or blender with the mint and process for 2 minutes. Dilute with chilled water.

Beet & Orange Juice

SERVES 1–2

Ingredients

1 whole, raw beet complete with leafy tops, if possible
3 large oranges
small piece fresh ginger
3–4 tbsp. mineral water, to blend (optional)
orange wedges, to decorate
chilled mineral water, to dilute (optional)

Method

Discard the root from the beet. Peel the beet as thinly as possible, cut into chunks, and reserve. Wash the beet leaves thoroughly and chop. Peel the oranges, discarding the bitter white pith and divide into segments. Peel the ginger and chop. Pass through a juicer or blender (adding a little water, if blending) until the juice is formed. Pour into glasses, decorate, and serve diluted with water, if liked.

Beet is a vegetable often overlooked, which is a great shame. Even more of a shame is that the leaves of the plant are nearly always thrown away—beet leaves provide an excellent source of calcium, iron, and beta-carotene.

ALTERNATIVE Omit the ginger and replace with 5 trimmed and chopped scallions and a few dashes of Worcestershire or Tabasco sauce for a more spicy flavor.

Pepper Medley

SERVES 1

Ingredients

1 red bell pepper
1 yellow bell pepper
1 orange bell pepper
1 jalapeño chile, seeded
1 large orange
few fresh parsley leaves, plus extra for decorating
chilled mineral water, to dilute (optional)
ice cubes, to serve (optional)

Method

Cut all the bell peppers into quarters and discard the seeds and inner membrane, then chop coarsely. Discard the seed membrane from the chile, then chop. Peel the orange, discarding the bitter white pith, and divide into segments. Pass all the ingredients (except the decoration, water, and ice) through a juicer or blender until the juice is formed, then dilute with the water, if using. Pour into the glass and add ice cubes, decorate, and serve.

Bell peppers are now as common to us as tomatoes, celery, or onions and are readily available in red, yellow, orange, or green. Having a sweet flavor, they combine well with most ingredients and are perhaps one of our most versatile vegetables.

ALTERNATIVE Omit the chile and use basil in place of the parsley. Process the bell peppers with a little iced water to form a juice. Pour into the glass and dilute with iced water, if liked.

Tomato & Celeriac Juice

SERVES 1

Ingredients

2 medium, fresh tomatoes
½ celeriac (celery root)
4 scallions, trimmed, plus extra for decoration
chilled mineral water, to dilute (optional)
2 celery stalks, to serve (optional)
ice cubes, to serve
cherry tomato, to decorate

Method

Lightly rinse the tomatoes, then chop coarsely. Peel the celeriac and cut into small chunks. Cut the scallions into small lengths. Pass all the vegetables through a juicer or blender until the juice is formed. Dilute with the water, if using. Pour into the glass, add a celery stalk for stirring, if using, add the ice cubes, decorate, and serve.

Look for plump, juicy tomatoes when juicing, because underripe tomatoes will produce an unsatisfactory result—little juice, with a tart flavor. However, do not be tempted to use damaged or overripe tomatoes because, although the yield will be good, the flavor could be impaired.

ALTERNATIVE Add a few dashes sweet chili or Tabasco sauce after juicing.

Watercress, Tomato & Leek Juice

SERVES 1

Ingredients

4 oz. watercress
2 medium, fresh ripe tomatoes
4 oz. tender leeks
1 medium orange
chilled mineral water, to dilute (optional)
cherry tomato and thyme sprig, to decorate

Method

Lightly rinse the watercress and reserve. Rinse the tomatoes, chop, and add to the watercress. Trim the leeks, chop coarsely, and wash thoroughly in cold water. Drain. Peel the orange, discarding the bitter white pith, and divide into segments. Pass through a juicer or blender until the juice is formed, then pour into the glass and dilute with the water, if using. Decorate and serve.

Watercress's clean peppery taste combines well with juicy tomatoes and leeks. It is recommended that young, tender leeks are used to produce the best results.

ALTERNATIVE Replace the watercress with arugula, sorrel, or spinach. Make sure that they are all thoroughly washed and shake vigorously before using.

Celery, Cucumber & Kiwi

SERVES 1

Ingredients

4 celery stalks
1 long English cucumber
2 green kiwi
chilled mineral water, to dilute (optional)
ice cubes, to serve
celery stalk, for stirring

Method

Trim the celery, removing the stringy threads, and chop coarsely. Peel the cucumber and discard the seeds, then chop coarsely. Scoop out the flesh from the kiwis. Pass all through a juicer or blender until the juice is formed, then dilute with the water, if using. Pour into the glass, add the ice cubes, and serve with the celery stalk for stirring.

This cool, green juice is perfect for any time of the day but most especially as a breakfast wake-up call. To get the maximum effect, ensure that you serve it chilled.

ALTERNATIVE Replace the kiwis with the flesh from 1 small melon, discarding the skin and seeds.

Tomato, Avocado & Scallion

SERVES 2

Ingredients

3 medium, fresh tomatoes
1 ripe avocado
3 tbsp. lime juice
4 scallions
chilled mineral water, to dilute
Worcestershire or Tabasco sauce, to serve
lime slices, to decorate

Method

Rinse the tomatoes and chop coarsely. Peel the avocado, discard the pit, chop into chunks, and toss in the lime juice. Trim the scallions and chop, then add to the tomatoes and avocado. Pass all the ingredients through a juicer or blender until the juice is formed. Dilute with the water. Pour into glasses and serve with Worcestershire or Tabasco sauce and lime slices.

This juice would make a perfect nonalcoholic cocktail. Serve with some Worcestershire or Tabasco sauce and a twist of lime for a refreshing start to any evening.

ALTERNATIVE Add a small amount of chile to the ingredients before blending. Be careful not to add too much—more can always be added if it is not spicy enough for your taste.

Tasty Treats & Summer Smoothies

Banana Latte

SERVES 2

This smooth, delicious drink may sound a little indulgent, but it is actually not too over the top. Use freshly brewed coffee made from fresh ground coffee beans instead of instant coffee.

Ingredients

⅔ cup whole or low-fat milk
1¼ cups freshly brewed coffee
2 ripe medium bananas
4–6 ice cubes
2 tbsp. low-fat crème fraîche or whipped cream, to serve
½ tsp. grated chocolate, to decorate

Method

Blend the milk and coffee together and reserve. Peel the bananas and cut into chunks. Place all the ingredients to be blended in a smoothie machine or blender. If using a smoothie machine, blend on mix for 15 seconds and then on smooth for 30 seconds. In a blender, blend for 1–2 minutes. Place the ice cubes in glasses, pour over the coffee mixture, top with the crème fraîche, and sprinkle with the grated chocolate.

ALTERNATIVE Replace the grated chocolate with a little grated cinnamon and, if you're counting the calories, omit crème fraîche or whipped cream.

Apple & Peach Smoothie

SERVES 1

Ingredients

2 red apples, such as Gala
2 tbsp. orange juice
2 ripe peaches
⅔ cup low-fat plain yogurt
ice cubes, to serve
orange wedge, to decorate

Method

Cut the apples into quarters and discard the core. Chop, then pour the orange juice over them and reserve. Peel the peaches, if preferred, cut in half, and discard the pits. Place all the ingredients to be blended in a smoothie machine or blender. If using a smoothie machine, blend on mix for 15 seconds and then on smooth for 30 seconds. In a blender, blend for 1–2 minutes. Pour into the glass, add the ice cubes, decorate, and serve.

When making this smoothie, do ensure that the peaches are ripe—if not, the flavor will be slightly impaired. Try using peach-flavor yogurt for a greater depth of flavor.

ALTERNATIVE If liked, add 1–2 drops almond extract and replace the yogurt with orange juice. You could also top the smoothies with a spoonful yogurt.

SERVES 2

Berry Smoothie

Ingredients

1 lb. mixed berries
1 large, ripe banana, peeled
6 tbsp. frozen strawberry yogurt
extra berries, to decorate

Method

Clean the fruits, cutting any larger fruits into halves or quarters. Place all the ingredients to be blended in a smoothie machine or blender. If using a smoothie machine, blend on mix for 15 seconds and then on smooth for 30 seconds. In a blender, blend for 1–2 minutes. Pour into tall glasses, decorate the glasses with the berries, and serve immediately.

Choose from a selection of mixed berries, such as strawberries, blueberries, raspberries, or blackberries. Do ensure that they are in peak condition, perfectly ripe, and fresh.

ALTERNATIVE Add 6 ice cubes to the berries and banana before blending and, once the ice is crushed, pour into tall glasses and top with a scoop of vanilla ice cream.

Tropical Delight

SERVES 1

Ingredients

1 large, ripe mango
1 large, ripe papaya
2 ripe bananas, peeled and cut into chunks
juice of ½ lime
2–3 tsp. honey
1¼ cups coconut milk
ice cubes, to serve
lime slice, to decorate

Method

Peel the mango and papaya and discard the pit and seeds. Chop the fruits into large chunks and pour over the lime juice, then place all the ingredients to be blended in a smoothie machine or blender. If using a smoothie machine, blend on mix for 15 seconds and then on smooth for 30 seconds. In a blender, blend for 1–2 minutes. Place some ice cubes into a tall glass and add the prepared drink. Decorate and serve immediately.

You can vary the fruits used in this smoothie, according to taste and availability. Ensure that the fruits are at their best—ripe and full of flavor and aroma.

ALTERNATIVE Replace the coconut milk with Greek yogurt and sprinkle the top with a little ground cinnamon.

Honeyed Figs with Yogurt

SERVES 1

Ingredients

4–6 fresh, ripe figs, depending on size
1¼ cups Greek yogurt
2–3 tsp. honey
1 tbsp. grated orange zest
4–6 ice cubes

Method

Cut the figs in half and scoop out the flesh and place all the ingredients to be blended in a smoothie machine or blender. If using a smoothie machine, blend on mix for 15 seconds and then on smooth for 30 seconds. In a blender, blend for 1–2 minutes. Pour into the glass and serve immediately.

There are hundreds of varieties of fig, varying in color from purple, green to almost white. Figs are at their best when fresh and ripe, bursting with flavor and aroma, in June through October. You can also buy them dried or semidried, but these would need a little cooking in some orange juice before using to make this smoothie.

ALTERNATIVE If fresh figs are not available, gently poach ⅔ cup chopped dried figs in ⅔ cup orange juice for 10 minutes, or until soft, then use instead of the fresh figs.

Passion Fruit & Guava Special

SERVES 1–2

Use passion fruit juice if fresh fruits are not available or you cannot wait for the fruits to ripen. Do not be tempted to use underripe fruits because the flavor will be seriously impaired.

Ingredients

2 ripe passion fruits
2 ripe guavas
2 Golden Delicious apples
4 scoops good-quality vanilla ice cream

Method

Scoop the flesh and seeds from the passion fruits and, if liked, strain to remove the seeds. Discard the seeds from the guavas. Cut the apples into quarters, discard the cores, and cut into wedges. Reserve 2 scoops of the ice cream, placing all the other ingredients in a smoothie machine or blender. If using a smoothie machine, blend on mix for 15 seconds and then on smooth for 30 seconds. In a blender, blend for 1–2 minutes. Pour into glasses, top with the remaining ice cream, and serve.

ALTERNATIVE Use 1 large, ripe orange in place of the apples, discarding the peel and bitter white pith before chopping into chunks.

Pineapple & Raspberry Smoothie

SERVES 1

Ingredients

1 medium, ripe pineapple
1¾ cups fresh raspberries
⅔ cup orange juice
6 ice cubes
1 tbsp. lightly whipped cream, to serve
1–2 tsp. grated semisweet chocolate, to decorate

This smoothie can be enjoyed all year round because both fruits are now readily available. If you happen to grow your own raspberries, this is a great recipe for using the fruits that are not perfect to look at but are ripe and bursting with the summer sun.

Method

Discard the plume and skin from the pineapple and cut lengthwise into quarters. Discard the hard central core and cut the flesh into chunks. Reserving 1 raspberry to decorate, place all the ingredients to be blended in a smoothie machine or blender. If using a smoothie machine, blend on mix for 15 seconds and then on smooth for 30 seconds. In a blender, blend for 1–2 minutes. Pour into the glass and top with the cream and raspberry. Sprinkle with the grated chocolate and serve immediately.

ALTERNATIVE Omit the orange juice and replace with coconut milk and sprinkle with a little toasted dry coconut.

Apricot Nectar

SERVES 1

When you are feeling like giving yourself an extra-special treat or just need to indulge, then this smoothie is perfect for you. Make and enjoy at leisure.

Ingredients

6 fresh ripe apricots
4 scoops good-quality vanilla ice cream
1¼ cups orange juice
1 tsp. toasted slivered almonds, to serve

Method

Lightly rinse the apricots, cut in half, and discard the pits. Reserve an apricot slice for decoration, if liked, as well as 2 scoops of the ice cream. Place all the other ingredients to be blended in a smoothie machine or blender. If using a smoothie machine, blend on mix for 15 seconds and then on smooth for 30 seconds. In a blender, blend for 1–2 minutes. Pour into the glass, top with the remaining ice cream, sprinkle with the slivered almonds, and serve.

ALTERNATIVE Use peaches or nectarines in place of the apricots and add 1–2 drops almond extract.

Cool Raspberry Soda

SERVES 2

Ingredients

1 lb. fresh raspberries
1–2 tsp. honey
4 tbsp. orange juice
6 ice cubes
club soda, to serve
2–4 scoops raspberry ripple ice cream, to serve

Method

Hull and clean the raspberries if necessary, reserving a few for decoration. Place all the ingredients to be blended in a smoothie machine or blender. If using a smoothie machine, blend on mix for 15 seconds and then on smooth for 30 seconds. In a blender, blend for 1–2 minutes. Pour into glasses, top off with club soda, add a scoop of ice cream to each, decorate, and serve immediately.

If you are fortunate enough to have a pick-your-own fruit farm near you, look for one of the many berries that are available in small outlets. You may find one of the more unusual berries not readily available in grocery stores, such as loganberries or boysenberries, which make a delicious substitute for the raspberries in this recipe.

ALTERNATIVE Replace the raspberries with fresh strawberries, cutting them in half, if large, and use strawberry ice cream.

Banana with Ginger Cream

SERVES 2

Ingredients

2 large, ripe bananas
2 large oranges
1¼ cups coconut milk
6 ice cubes
2 tbsp. whipped heavy cream, to serve
1 tsp. grated fresh or ground ginger, to decorate
1 tsp. candied ginger, chopped, to decorate

Method

Peel the bananas and cut into chunks. Peel the oranges, discard the pith, and divide into segments. Place all the ingredients to be blended, including the ice, in a smoothie machine or blender. If using a smoothie machine, blend on mix for 15 seconds and then on smooth for 30 seconds. In a blender, blend for 1–2 minutes. Mix the cream and ginger together and stir half into the drink. Pour into glasses, top with the remaining cream and the candied ginger, and serve.

There are many forms of ginger available, ranging from fresh ginger and ground ginger to preserved and candied ginger, which are far sweeter. Use whichever you prefer when making the cream for this recipe.

ALTERNATIVE Replace 1 of the bananas with 1 cup peeled and pitted litchis.

Apricot & Passion Fruit Lassi

SERVES 2

Ingredients

6 ripe apricots
2 ripe passion fruits
⅔ cup litchis
⅔ cup plain yogurt
⅔ cup apple juice
6 ice cubes
2 lime slices, to decorate

Method

Lightly rinse the apricots and cut in half, discarding the pits. Cut the passion fruits in half and scoop out the seeds and flesh. Strain the flesh, if preferred. Peel and pit the litchis, then place all the ingredients (including the ice cubes) in a smoothie machine or blender. If using a smoothie machine, blend on mix for 15 seconds and then on smooth for 30 seconds. In a blender, blend for 1–2 minutes. Pour into glasses, decorate, and serve immediately.

Apricots originate from China but are now widely available when in season. This recipe blends lush, fresh apricots with litchis, aromatic passion fruits, and plain yogurt, resulting in an absolutely fabulous drink.

ALTERNATIVE Replace the litchis with 1 ripe, peeled banana. If liked, use Greek yogurt in place of the plain yogurt.

Honeyed Banana Soda

SERVES 1

Ingredients

2 large, ripe bananas
2 tbsp. freshly squeezed orange juice
1 tbsp. honey
1¼ cups coconut milk
2 ice cubes
½ tsp. freshly grated nutmeg
club soda, to serve

Method

Peel and chop the bananas and pour the orange juice over them. Place all the ingredients except the club soda in a smoothie machine or blender. If using a smoothie machine, blend on mix for 15 seconds and then on smooth for 30 seconds. In a blender, blend for 1–2 minutes. Pour into the glass, add a little club soda to dilute, and serve.

When using honey in cooking, whether it is in drinks, desserts, or savory dishes, always use liquid honey unless the recipe states otherwise. It is far easier to pour and blends quickly with the other ingredients.

ALTERNATIVE Replace the coconut milk with plain yogurt and use ground cinnamon in place of the nutmeg. Add a long cinnamon stick for stirring.

Raspberry Pavlova

SERVES 2

Ingredients

1¾ cups fresh or thawed frozen raspberries
1 cup whole or low-fat milk
2 scoops vanilla ice cream
2 tbsp. lightly whipped cream, to serve
2–4 tiny meringues, to serve
2 chocolate-filled rolled wafer cookies, to serve

Method

Place the raspberries, milk, and ice cream in a smoothie machine or blender. If using a smoothie machine, blend on mix for 15 seconds and then on smooth for 30 seconds. In a blender, blend for 1–2 minutes. Pour into glasses, top with the whipped cream, and crumble over the meringues. Serve immediately with the wafers.

This recipe is based on the very popular dessert of the same name and provides a delicious indulgence, something we all need occasionally. Try it and see.

ALTERNATIVE Use other fruits in place of the raspberries—try fresh ripe peaches, nectarines, strawberries, or blueberries.

Lemon Meringue Shake

SERVES 2

Ingredients

1 tbsp. finely grated lemon zest
⅓ cup freshly squeezed lemon juice
1–2 tbsp. honey, or to taste
2 cups whole or low-fat milk
2–4 scoops lemon sorbet
2 tbsp. lightly whipped cream, to serve
2 small meringues, to decorate
thinly pared lemon zest, to decorate

Method

Place the lemon zest and juice in a smoothie machine or blender and add the honey, milk, and sorbet. Blend for 45 seconds to 1 minute, or until smooth. Pour into glasses and top with the cream. Crumble the meringues and sprinkle over the top, then serve, decorated with the pared lemon zest.

When using the zest from citrus fruits, wherever possible use organic fruits because these have not been sprayed with chemicals. Organic or not, it is still important that the fruits are thoroughly washed before using the zest.

ALTERNATIVE Replace the lemon with orange or lime, or even use all three. Raspberries would also work well, especially if combined with raspberry sorbet.

Orange Flip

SERVES 1

Ingredients

2 large eggs
2–3 tsp. honey
1¼ cups freshly squeezed orange juice
2 tbsp. freshly squeezed lemon juice
6 ice cubes
orange slice, to decorate

Be careful when selecting the eggs for this recipe. Use eggs that are as fresh as possible and, before use, store either in their box or in the egg compartment of the refrigerator. Let them reach room temperature for 30 minutes before using. If you are pregnant or have recently recovered from illness, it is recommended that you do not make this drink.

Method

Place all the ingredients in a smoothie machine or blender. If using a smoothie machine, blend on mix for 15 seconds and then on smooth for 30 seconds. In a blender, blend for 1–2 minutes. Pour into the glass, decorate, and serve immediately.

ALTERNATIVE Replace the orange juice with 1¼ cups black currant juice and top with a spoonful of whipped cream.

Pineapple Smoothie

SERVES 1

Ingredients

1 medium, ripe pineapple
2 ripe passion fruits, flesh and seeds scooped out
1 large, ripe banana, peeled and cut into chunks
1¼ cups plain yogurt
2–3 tsp. honey
4 ice cubes
2 scoops vanilla ice cream, to serve
1 tsp. grated milk chocolate, to decorate
maraschino cherry, to decorate

Method

Discard the plume, skin, and hard core of the pineapple and cut into chunks. Reserve a little for decoration. Place all the ingredients to be blended, including the ice, in a smoothie machine or blender. If using a smoothie machine, blend on mix for 15 seconds and then on smooth for 30 seconds. In a blender, blend for 1–2 minutes. Pour into the glass, top with the ice cream, decorate, and serve.

For this smoothie, you can use either fresh pineapple or pineapple juice; the choice is yours, depending on whether you prefer a smooth drink or if you like the pieces of fruit.

ALTERNATIVE Replace the passion fruits with strawberries and use strawberry-flavor yogurt.

Strawberry Delight

SERVES 2

Ingredients

11 oz. fresh, ripe strawberries
few shakes freshly ground black pepper
⅔ cup strawberry yogurt
⅔ cup plain yogurt
2–4 scoops vanilla ice cream
2 tbsp. whipped cream, to serve
strawberry fans and mint sprigs, to decorate (optional)

Method

Hull, then lightly rinse the strawberries and, if large, cut in half. Place all the ingredients to be blended, including the scoops of ice cream, in a smoothie machine or blender. If using a smoothie machine, blend on mix for 15 seconds and then on smooth for 30 seconds. In a blender, blend for 1–2 minutes. Pour into glasses and top with the cream. Decorate each with a strawberry fan and mint sprig, if using.

If possible, use locally grown strawberries, because they usually have more flavor than fruit that has been packaged in a supermarket. Try to avoid keeping strawberries in the refrigerator, but, if you have to, remove them at least 30 minutes before using.

ALTERNATIVE Using freshly ground black pepper with strawberries helps to bring out the flavor. A few drops of balsamic vinegar also has the same effect. If preferred, use a little honey.

Apple Crumble Smoothie

SERVES 2

Replace a favorite dessert with a smoothie that is simple to prepare, ready in minutes, and tastes fantastic. Other fruits can be used instead of apple, much as you can substitute the fruits in baked desserts.

Ingredients

3 sweet, juicy apples
2 tsp. finely grated orange zest
⅓ cup apple juice
1¼ cups plain yogurt
⅔ cup fresh custard
2–4 scoops vanilla ice cream, to serve
2 cookies, halved, to serve
1 tbsp. toasted, crushed slivered almonds and strawberry, to decorate

Method

Cut the apples into quarters and discard the cores. Chop into chunks and place all the ingredients to be blended in a smoothie machine or blender. If using a smoothie machine, blend on mix for 15 seconds and then on smooth for 30 seconds. In a blender, blend for 1–2 minutes. Pour into glasses and top with the ice cream. Place the cookies in the ice cream, sprinkle with the almonds, decorate, and serve.

ALTERNATIVE Replace the cookies with a crumbled granola bar.

Cherry Jubilee

SERVES 2

Ingredients

2 cups pitted, fresh, ripe cherries
⅓ cup apple juice
1¼ cups cherry-flavored yogurt
6 ice cubes
2 tbsp. whipped cream, to serve
extra cherries and mint sprigs, to decorate

Method

Place all the ingredients to be blended, including the ice cubes, in a smoothie machine or blender. If using a smoothie machine, blend on mix for 15 seconds and then on smooth for 30 seconds. In a blender, blend for 1–2 minutes. Pour into glasses, top with the cream, and decorate with the cherries and mint sprigs.

Cherries are one of the fruits that are only obtainable seasonally, so, when they are around, make the most of them. Although it is not possible to buy frozen cherries, they do freeze reasonably well, so, when in season, buy more than you need and freeze some.

ALTERNATIVE Replace the cherries with blackberries and decorate with whole blackberries.

Aromatic Mango Lassi

SERVES 2

Aromatic spices are widely available in most supermarkets, so add a touch of Asia to your smoothie. When buying spices, unless you use them often, buy in small quantities, because their aroma and flavor do not last for long. Store them away from the light in airtight containers.

Ingredients

2 large, ripe mangoes
4 cardamom pods
1 small piece star anise
2 tsp. honey
⅔ cup apple juice
⅔ cup coconut milk
⅔ cup plain yogurt
lime wedges, to decorate
cinnamon stick, to stir (optional)

Method

Peel the mangoes, cut the flesh away from the pits, cut the flesh into chunks, and reserve. Crush the cardamom pods, remove the seeds, and discard the pods. Finely crush the star anise. Place all the ingredients to be blended in a smoothie machine or blender. If using a smoothie machine, blend on mix for 15 seconds and then on smooth for 30 seconds. In a blender, blend for 1–2 minutes. Pour into glasses, decorate, and serve with the cinnamon stick to stir, if using.

ALTERNATIVE Replace the mango with papaya and use orange juice instead of apple.

Banana & Raspberry Smoothie

SERVES 1

Ingredients

2 ripe bananas
1¾ cups fresh raspberries
3 oz. tofu, drained
⅔ cup orange juice
4 ice cubes

Method

Peel the bananas and cut into chunks. Place the bananas in a smoothie machine or blender. Reserve a raspberry for decoration, then place all the remaining ingredients into the smoothie machine or blender. If using a smoothie machine, blend on mix for 15 seconds and then on smooth for 45 seconds. In a blender, blend for 1–2 minutes until smooth. Pour into the glass, decorate, and serve.

This nourishing smoothie will help sustain you throughout the day. Not only is it full of energy-rich fruits, it also contains tofu, which will keep you feeling energized.

ALTERNATIVE Other fruits can be used in place of the raspberries—try blueberries, blackberries, or loganberries.

Peanut Butter Bliss

SERVES 1

It is your choice whether you use chunky peanut butter or smooth in this recipe. Although relatively high in calories, an occasional treat is a good idea, because it helps to lift the spirits and give a general feeling of well-being. Nuts also contain important nutrients.

Ingredients

4 tbsp. orange juice
3 tbsp. chunky or smooth peanut butter
1 ripe banana, chopped
2 tbsp. lemon juice
2 scoops chocolate ice cream
1 scoop vanilla ice cream, to serve
wafer cookie, to serve

Method

Place the orange juice, peanut butter, banana, lemon juice, and chocolate ice cream in a smoothie machine or blender. If using a smoothie machine, blend on mix for 15 seconds and then on smooth for 45 seconds. In a blender, blend for 1–2 minutes until smooth. Pour into the glass, add a scoop of vanilla ice cream, and top with a wafer cookie. Serve immediately.

ALTERNATIVE Replace the ice cream with scoops of frozen strawberry yogurt or raspberry sorbet and add a few fresh strawberries or raspberries to the machine prior to blending.

Frosty Fruit Smoothie

SERVES 2

During the summer months when a cold, frosty smoothie is called for, it is a good idea to keep a variety of fruits in the refrigerator, so that a refreshing drink can be blended in seconds.

Ingredients

1 cup chilled seedless green grapes
2 ripe passion fruits
½ ripe galia or cantaloupe melon, chilled
⅔ cup chilled apple juice
4 ice cubes

Method

Rinse the grapes and discard any stalks. Reserve a few for decoration and place the rest in a smoothie machine or blender. Scoop the flesh and seeds from the passion fruits, sieve if a smooth texture is preferred and add to the machine. Discard the skin and seeds from the melon and cut into chunks. Place all the remaining ingredients in the machine. Blend in a smoothie machine on mix for 15 seconds and then on smooth for 45 seconds. In a blender, blend for 1–2 minutes until smooth. Pour into cold glasses, decorate, and serve.

ALTERNATIVE Other chilled juices can be used in place of the apple juice. Apple and cranberry or apple and mango juice work particularly well.

Tropical Fruit Smoothie

SERVES 2

Ingredients

1 large, ripe avocado
2 tbsp. lime juice
1 medium, ripe pineapple
1 tsp. clear honey
⅔ cup chilled coconut milk
4 ice cubes
2–4 scoops chocolate ice cream, to serve

Method

Peel the avocado, discard the pit, cut the flesh into chunks, and sprinkle with the lime juice. Cut the plume and skin off the pineapple and discard. Cut into quarters and discard the hard central core. Cut the flesh into chunks. Place all the ingredients except the ice cream in a smoothie machine or blender. If using a smoothie machine, blend on mix for 15 seconds and then on smooth for 45 seconds. In a blender, blend for 1–2 minutes until smooth. Pour into glasses, top with the ice cream, and serve immediately.

Pineapple contains bromelain, which helps to balance the acidity and alkalinity levels in the digestive system. Although coconut milk contains saturated fat, research indicates that it is not nearly as harmful as fat from animal and dairy products.

ALTERNATIVE Omit the pineapple and use any other tropical fruits instead. Papayas, passion fruits, or mangoes would all work well in this recipe.

Chilled Apple & Blackberry Smoothie

SERVES 1–2

Ingredients

2 ripe apples
4 tbsp. apple juice
1 cup chilled or frozen ripe blackberries, plus a few extra for decoration
1¼ cups plain yogurt
2–4 mint sprigs, plus 2–4 more to decorate
2–4 scoops caramel pecan or vanilla ice cream, to serve
2–4 ripe blackberries or 2–4 apple wedges, to decorate

Method

Rinse the apples, core, and cut into chunks. Place the apple juice, chopped apples, blackberries, yogurt, and mint in a smoothie machine or blender. If using a smoothie machine, blend on mix for 15 seconds, then switch to smooth for 45 seconds. In a blender, blend for 1–2 minutes until smooth. Pour into glasses, top with the ice cream, and decorate with the remaining mint sprigs and ripe blackberries.

Apples are universally popular and have definite health properties. They are full of vitamin C with a low glycemia index, which help to keep hunger pangs at bay.

ALTERNATIVE Raspberries or strawberries can replace the blackberries. If using strawberries, chill instead of freezing, but the raspberries can be chilled or frozen.

Strawberry Slush

SERVES 2

Ingredients

1 lb. fresh strawberries, hulled
1 tbsp. balsamic vinegar
3 tbsp. orange juice
4 ice cubes
2–4 mint sprigs, to decorate

Strawberries are now readily available all year round, coming from many countries worldwide. When locally grown strawberries are available, use these, however, because the flavor will be far superior to those that have been picked slightly underripe. Locally grown berries are allowed to ripen on the plant, thus enjoying more of the sun, and have much more flavor.

Method

Lightly rinse the strawberries and reserve 2–4 for decoration. Let the remaining strawberries drain. Spread on a baking sheet, sprinkle with the balsamic vinegar, and let stand for at least 5 minutes. Place the strawberries and any juice together with the orange juice and ice cubes in a smoothie machine or blender. If using a smoothie machine, blend on mix for 15 seconds and then on smooth for 45 seconds. In a blender, blend for 1–2 minutes until smooth and a "slush" is formed. Pour into glasses, decorate, and serve immediately.

ALTERNATIVE Look for white balsamic vinegar in place of the traditional balsamic vinegar, or use a few twists of freshly ground black pepper instead.

Pear & Maple Swirl

SERVES 1

This delicious smoothie can be mixed and matched according to personal tastes. We all need a little indulgence occasionally and the maple syrup adds that finishing touch.

Ingredients

2 large, ripe dessert pears, such as William or Conference
1 tsp. finely grated orange zest
1¼ cups live plain yogurt
1–2 scoops caramel-flavor or vanilla ice cream
orange zest, to decorate
1–2 tbsp. maple syrup, to serve

Method

Peel and core the pears, chop, and place in a smoothie machine or blender with the orange zest and yogurt. If using a smoothie machine, blend on mix for 15 seconds, then switch to smooth for 45 seconds, or blend in a blender for 1–2 minutes until smooth. Pour into the glass, top with the ice cream, and decorate with the orange zest. Swirl with a little maple syrup and serve immediately.

ALTERNATIVE Use chocolate ice cream and swirl with a little melted white chocolate.

Eastern Delight

SERVES 2

Ingredients

1¼ cups coconut milk
14 oz. canned litchis, drained
2 cardamom pods
1 lemongrass stalk
1 small piece star anise
2–4 scoops vanilla ice cream, to serve
2 lemon slices, to decorate

Method

Place the coconut milk with the drained fruits in a smoothie machine or blender. Place the cardamom pods in a mortar and pound with a pestle to remove the seeds. Place the seeds in the machine. Remove the outer leaves from the lemongrass, chop, then pound with the star anise until as fine as possible. Add to the machine. If using a smoothie machine, blend on mix for 15 seconds and then on smooth for 45 seconds. In a blender, blend for 1–2 minutes until smooth. Pour into glasses, top with the ice cream, decorate, and serve.

Canned litchis are blended with Eastern spices in this recipe to make an aromatic smoothie with a hint of Asia.

ALTERNATIVE You will find that the small pieces of spice will sink to the bottom of the drink, but you can strain the liquid, if liked. Use plain yogurt in place of the coconut milk, if preferred.

Rhubarb & Ginger Smoothie

SERVES 2

Ingredients

12 oz. rhubarb
⅓ cup ginger wine
1–2 tbsp., or to taste, honey
1¼ cups freshly made custard
½ tsp. powdered ginger
2–4 scoops vanilla ice cream
¼ tsp. ground cinnamon, to decorate

Method

Trim the rhubarb and cut into chunks. Place all the ingredients except the ice cream in a smoothie machine or blender. If using a smoothie machine, blend on mix for 15 seconds and then on smooth for 45 seconds. In a blender, blend for 1–2 minutes until smooth. Pour into glasses, top each with a scoop of ice cream, sprinkle with the ground cinnamon, and serve.

Rhubarb is rich in calcium, but the acidic content in the fruit can hinder its absorption. Add a little ginger, honey, or sugar to counteract the tartness and help with the absorption. Only use the stalks, never the leaves. Strawberries and rhubarb is a popular combination.

ALTERNATIVE Use 14 oz. canned rhubarb, drained, and omit the ginger wine. Add honey to taste, if liked, and top with a little chopped preserved ginger.

Almond, Plum & Strawberry Smoothie

SERVES 1–2

Ingredients

8 oz. ripe plums
1¼ cups strawberry yogurt
few drops almond extract
2–3 tsp. honey, or to taste
1–2 scoops strawberry or vanilla ice cream, to serve
1 tbsp. toasted slivered almonds, to decorate
1–2 strawberry slices, to decorate

Method

Rinse the plums, cut in half, discard the pits, and place in a smoothie machine or blender. Spoon the yogurt into the machine and add the almond extract and honey to taste. If using a smoothie machine, blend on mix for 15 seconds and then on smooth for 45 seconds. In a blender, blend for 1–2 minutes until smooth. Pour into glasses, add a scoop of ice cream to each, sprinkle with the toasted slivered almonds, decorate with the strawberry slices, and serve.

Plums offer a good source of fiber. Red plums also contain beta-carotene—the pigment found in such foods as carrots, oranges, and dark green vegetables—and an important antioxidant nutrient.

ALTERNATIVE If fresh plums are not available, use 14 oz. canned plums. Drain well and then proceed as above.

Banana Sundae Smoothie

SERVES 2

When using bananas in smoothies, do ensure that they are ripe. Underripe fruit will not blend well with the other ingredients, and the flavor will be impaired.

Ingredients

2 ripe bananas
⅔ cup freshly squeezed orange juice
1¼ cups coconut milk
4 fresh or dried dates, pitted and chopped
2 scoops chocolate ice cream, to serve
2–4 ripe or maraschino cherries, to serve
1 tsp. grated chocolate, to decorate

Method

Cut the bananas into chunks and place all the ingredients except the ice cream, the cherries, and chocolate in a smoothie machine or blender. If using a smoothie machine, blend on mix for 15 seconds and then on smooth for 45 seconds. In a blender, blend for 1–2 minutes until smooth. Pour into glasses and add a scoop of ice cream to each. Decorate with the cherries and a sprinkle of chocolate and serve.

ALTERNATIVE Replace the coconut milk with strawberry-flavor yogurt and use caramel pecan ice cream.

Passionate Peach Melba Smoothie

SERVES 2

Ingredients

1 ripe passion fruit
3 tbsp. mango or orange juice
3–4 ripe peaches, pitted
1½ cups fresh or thawed frozen raspberries
4 scoops vanilla ice cream
2 peach wedges, to decorate
wafer cookies, to serve

Method

Cut the passion fruit in half and scoop out the flesh and seeds. Strain the flesh if a smoother texture is preferred. Place in a smoothie machine or blender and add the mango or orange juice, peaches, raspberries (reserving 4 or so for decoration), and 2 scoops ice cream. If using a smoothie machine, blend on mix for 15 seconds and then on smooth for 45 seconds. In a blender, blend for 1–2 minutes until smooth. Pour into glasses, add a scoop of ice cream to each, decorate, and serve.

Like the dessert of the same name, this smoothie is quick and easy to make and tastes even better than it looks. As with all smoothies, it is important to ensure that the fruit you use is in peak condition.

ALTERNATIVE Make the smoothie as above, omitting the raspberries but adding more peaches and a little more ice cream. Top with the ice cream, drizzle with raspberry coulis, and serve immediately.

SERVES 2

Real Strawberry Milkshake

Whether or not this transports you back to childhood, once tasted, this fabulous shake will have you hooked.

Ingredients

8 oz. ripe strawberries, plus 2 extra ripe strawberries to decorate
1¼ cups chilled low-fat milk
4 ice cubes
2 scoops strawberry-flavor ice cream, to serve
1 tbsp. lightly whipped heavy cream, to serve
mint sprigs, to decorate

Method

Hull the strawberries and rinse lightly. Place in a smoothie machine or blender and add the milk and ice cubes. If using a smoothie machine, blend on mix for 15 seconds and then on smooth for 45 seconds. In a blender, blend for 1–2 minutes until smooth. Pour into tall glasses and add a scoop of ice cream to each, top with a little whipped cream, and decorate with the extra strawberries and mint sprigs.

ALTERNATIVE Other fruits can be used. Try bananas, raspberries, apricots, or pineapple, varying the flavor of ice cream accordingly; or make a chocolate milkshake by omitting the fruits and using 2–3 tablespoons melted chocolate.

Black Currant Granita

SERVES 2

Ingredients

2 cups fresh black currants
⅔ cup fresh red currants
4 tbsp. black currant syrup or juice
2–3 tsp. honey, or to taste
1 large, or 2 medium, juicy apples, such as Granny Smith
6 ice cubes
orange zest and mint sprigs, to decorate

Method

Remove the stalks from the currants and rinse. Place them with the syrup and honey to taste in a smoothie machine or blender. Core the apples and cut into wedges. Add to the machine with the ice. If using a smoothie machine, blend on mix for 15 seconds and then on smooth for 45 seconds. In a blender, blend for 1–2 minutes until smooth. Pour into a freezeable container and freeze for 1 hour, or until slushy. Spoon into glasses, decorate, and serve immediately.

When making this granita, put the container in the coldest part of your freezer. Fresh currants are difficult to find, but if you can get them locally in your state, or grow them yourself, you'll appreciate them in this refreshing drink.

ALTERNATIVE Use only black currants, adjusting the measurement to 2⅔ cups. Add honey to taste.

Greek Delight

SERVES 2

Ingredients

4 ripe figs
2–3 tsp. honey, or to taste
2 large oranges
⅔ cup Greek yogurt
⅔ cup low-fat milk
2 scoops vanilla ice cream, to serve
2 mint sprigs, to decorate

Method

Lightly rinse the figs and cut in half, then place in a smoothie machine or blender with honey to taste. Peel the oranges, discarding the bitter white pith, and divide into segments. Add to the machine. Add the yogurt and milk. If using a smoothie machine, blend on mix for 15 seconds and then on smooth for 45 seconds. In a blender, blend for 1–2 minutes until smooth. Pour into glasses, add a scoop of ice cream to each, and decorate with the mint sprigs. Serve immediately.

Enjoy a taste of the Mediterranean sun with Greek yogurt and plump, lush purple or green figs. There is no need to skin these, but do use ripe fruits and, if necessary, let ripen for a couple of days in a warm room.

ALTERNATIVE Use ⅔ cup freshly squeezed orange juice in place of the whole oranges.

Caramel & Chocolate Smoothie

SERVES 2

Ingredients

1¼ cups caramel-flavor yogurt
⅔ cup chilled low-fat milk
4 scoops vanilla ice cream
2 wafer cookies, to serve
1 tsp. grated chocolate , to decorate

Method

Place the yogurt, milk, and 2 scoops of the ice cream in a smoothie machine or blender. If using a smoothie machine, blend on mix for 15 seconds and then on smooth for 45 seconds. In a blender, blend for 1–2 minutes until smooth. Pour into chilled glasses and add the remaining scoop of ice cream to each, along with a wafer cookie. Sprinkle with the grated chocolate and serve.

This is definitely an indulgent smoothie—so have it in the summer when you can go for a walk to work off the excess calories.

ALTERNATIVE Use a different flavor yogurt in place of the caramel—try raspberry, cherry, peach, or strawberry.

Detoxing & Revitalizing

Breakfast Smoothie

SERVES 1

Ingredients

1 large banana
1¼ cups freshly squeezed orange juice
4 ice cubes
1 tbsp. wheat germ
orange wedge, to decorate

Method

Peel the banana and add to the smoothie machine or blender with the other ingredients. If using a smoothie machine, blend on mix for 15 seconds and then on smooth for 45 seconds. In a blender, blend for 1–2 minutes until smooth. Pour into the glass, decorate, and serve.

Breakfast is the most important meal, preparing you for the rest of the day. Eating the right food for breakfast will stop you from being tempted by those mid-morning snacks. The wheat germ in this recipe is an excellent source of folic acid and vitamin E, which protects cell membranes and prevents the buildup of plaque in the arteries. Try it in place of coffee or tea.

ALTERNATIVE Replace the orange juice with 1 peeled and segmented whole orange.

Pick-Me-Up Smoothie

SERVES 2

Ingredients

2 apples
⅔ cup probiotic bio live plain yogurt
1¼ cups apple juice
heaping 2 tsp. wheatgrass powder
4 ice cubes

Method

Cut the apples into quarters, core, and chop. Place in a smoothie machine or blender with the yogurt, apple juice, wheatgrass, and ice cubes. If using a smoothie machine, blend on mix for 15 seconds and then on smooth for 45 seconds. In a blender, blend for 1–2 minutes until smooth. Pour into glasses and serve.

If you feel that you are in need of a good pick-me-up, then this smoothie is for you. It contains wheatgrass, an antioxidant with many other health benefits. This smoothie is excellent for vegetarians, because it contains all the B vitamins.

ALTERNATIVE Replace the apple juice with freshly brewed nettle tea, or, if available, add a small handful of fresh, rinsed nettles and filtered water instead of the nettle tea before blending.

Watermelon & Flax Oil Smoothie

SERVES 1

Flaxseed is available in capsule form as well as oil, and is a rich source of omega-3 fatty acids. One flaxseed capsule will provide the body's daily requirement.

Ingredients

2 large oranges
2 cups watermelon chunks, skin and seeds discarded
2 tbsp. flax oil
orange wedge, to decorate

Method

Peel the oranges, discarding the bitter white pith, then cut into chunks. Place the orange and watermelon chunks in a smoothie machine or blender and add the flax oil. If using a smoothie machine, blend on mix for 15 seconds and then on smooth for 45 seconds. In a blender, blend for 1–2 minutes until smooth. Pour into the glass, decorate, and serve.

ALTERNATIVE Use honeydew or galia melon if a watermelon is not available.

Herb Special

SERVES 1

Ingredients

small handful dandelion leaves
small handful lovage leaves
1 English cucumber
1¼ cups dandelion and burdock drink
6 ice cubes (made using filtered water)

Method

Thoroughly wash all the herbs and pat dry. Place in a smoothie machine or blender. Peel the cucumber and discard the seeds. Cut 1 slice to use for decoration, cut the rest into chunks, and add to the leaves, together with the liquid and ice cubes. If using a smoothie machine, blend on mix for 15 seconds and then on smooth for 45 seconds. In a blender, blend for 1–2 minutes until smooth. Pour into the glass, decorate, and serve immediately.

It has long been accepted that herbs can have a beneficial effect on the body and can be used in many cases to both heal and promote general well-being. So, when on a detox diet, do not overlook herbs. This drink will help eliminate fluid from the body—dandelions are a strong diuretic and good for detoxing of the blood as well as the liver.

ALTERNATIVE If this is a little bitter for your taste buds, replace the dandelion and burdock with freshly squeezed orange juice and, if still too bitter, a small squeeze of honey.

Carrot & Parsley Smoothie

SERVES 2

Ingredients

3 medium carrots, peeled
2 apples, cored
1 English cucumber
⅔ cup dandelion and burdock drink
small handful parsley, rinsed
few dandelion leaves, rinsed
⅔ cup live plain yogurt
parsley sprig, to decorate

Method

Cut the carrots and apples into chunks and place in a smoothie machine or blender. Peel the cucumber and discard the seeds. Cut 2 slices to use for decoration, chop the rest, and place in the machine. Add the dandelion and burdock drink, parsley, and dandelion leaves with the yogurt. If using a smoothie machine, blend on mix for 15 seconds and then on smooth for 45 seconds. In a blender, blend for 1–2 minutes until smooth. Pour into glasses, decorate, and serve.

Parsley is a good diuretic; it stimulates the liver and is rich in vitamin C. Try this smoothie if you have overdone the alcohol and have woken up feeling under the weather. If you are feeling organized, you could collect the ingredients before you go out in the evening and just quickly blend them together in the morning.

ALTERNATIVE Replace the dandelion and burdock with green tea and add some milk thistle and burdock leaves, if available.

Tomato, Celery & Marigold Smoothie

SERVES 2

Both the flower and leaves of the marigold can be eaten, but do make sure that you wash both thoroughly before use. Marigold is good for cleansing the lymphatic system, liver, and gallbladder as well as for improving circulation.

Ingredients

2 medium, ripe tomatoes
2 apples, cored
1 zucchini, peeled
few marigold flower heads and leaves
⅔ cup unsweetened apple juice
4 ice cubes
2 extra marigold flowers, if available, or cherry tomatoes, to decorate
celery stalk, to stir

Method

Cut the tomatoes, apple, and zucchini into chunks and place in a smoothie machine or blender with the marigold flowers and leaves. Add the apple juice and ice cubes. If using a smoothie machine, blend on mix for 15 seconds and then on smooth for 45 seconds. In a blender, blend for 1–2 minutes until smooth. Pour into glasses, decorate, and serve with a celery stalk for stirring.

ALTERNATIVE Replace the marigold flowers and leaves with 2–3 sprigs fresh thyme, which is also good for improving circulation.

Watermelon with Kiwi & Echinacea

SERVES 1

Ingredients

1 large wedge watermelon
3 kiwis
few drops echinacea tincture
1–2 tsp. finely grated orange zest
4 ice cubes
kiwi slice, to decorate

Method

Discard the skin and seeds from the watermelon, cut the flesh into chunks, and place in a smoothie machine or blender. Scoop the flesh from the kiwi fruits into the machine and add the echinacea, orange zest, and ice cubes. If using a smoothie machine, blend on mix for 15 seconds and then on smooth for 45 seconds. In a blender, blend for 1–2 minutes until smooth. Pour into the glass, decorate, and serve.

Echinacea is well known for helping the immune system, but it can also be used to stimulate the lymph glands, help the circulation, and to purify the blood.

ALTERNATIVE Add the peeled and segmented flesh from 1 large orange and add a small handful chives to help purify the blood.

Banana with Strawberries & Angelica

SERVES 2

Ingredients

2 large, ripe bananas
12 oz. strawberries
small piece fresh angelica stem or a few seeds and a couple leaves
⅔ cup green tea
1 tbsp. rolled oats
4 ice cubes
strawberries and mint sprigs, to decorate

Method

Peel and chop the bananas and cut the strawberries in half if large. Place in a smoothie machine or blender with the chopped angelica, tea, oats, and ice cubes. If using a smoothie machine, blend on mix for 15 seconds and then on smooth for 45 seconds. In a blender, blend for 1–2 minutes until smooth. Pour into glasses, decorate, and serve.

When using angelica, use washed and dried fresh leaves, seeds, or stem, not the candied variety. Angelica tends to be overlooked these days and relegated to the decoration of cakes and desserts. However, if you are lucky enough to have a plant, use the fresh leaves and stems in this delicious drink—it is good for stimulating the circulation and as a digestive and expectorant.

ALTERNATIVE Omit the bananas and use twice the weight of strawberries, adding an extra tablespoon rolled oats.

Fennel & Orange with Aloe Vera

SERVES 2

Ingredients

1 large Florence fennel bulb
2 large oranges, peeled and segmented
½ English cucumber
4 tbsp. aloe vera juice
1–2 shakes cayenne pepper
8 ice cubes
cucumber slices, to decorate

Method

Thoroughly wash the fennel and cut into chunks. Place in a smoothie machine or blender, together with the peeled and segmented oranges. Peel the cucumber, discard the seeds, then chop. Add to the machine with the aloe vera juice, cayenne pepper, and ice cubes. If using a smoothie machine, blend on mix for 15 seconds and then on smooth for 45 seconds. In a blender, blend for 1–2 minutes until smooth. Pour into glasses, decorate, and serve.

Aloe vera has been used throughout the ages to treat infections, allergies, and inflammation. It has also been used in treatment for chronic fatigue syndrome (CFS), candida, and in detoxification. It can be used both orally, as here, and applied to the skin.

ALTERNATIVE Replace the fennel bulb with a head of celery, trimming the stalks and washing thoroughly before use. Reserve the smaller celery stalks with leaves and use to stir the drink.

Fruit Salad Detox Smoothie

SERVES 1

As well as following a detox diet, for maximum benefit it is important to exercise on a regular basis. This helps to increase lymph gland activity and speed up the detox.

Ingredients

⅔ cup orange juice
1 apple
1 ripe peach
small melon wedge
few spinach leaves
small handful Italian flat-leaf parsley
6 ice cubes
parsley sprig and orange wedgc, to decorate

Method

Place the orange juice in a smoothie machine or blender. Core the apple and discard the peach pit. Discard the melon skin and seeds. Cut all the fruits into chunks and add to the orange juice with the spinach, parsley, and ice cubes. If using a smoothie machine, blend on mix for 15 seconds and then on smooth for 45 seconds. In a blender, blend for 1–2 minutes until smooth. Pour into the glass, decorate, and serve.

ALTERNATIVE Replace the spinach with arugula or sorrel leaves.

Tomato with Watermelon & Thyme

SERVES 1

Ingredients

2 medium, ripe tomatoes
4 tbsp. freshly brewed green tea
1 large wedge watermelon
small handful fresh thyme, plus sprig to decorate
few whole chive leaves
2–4 ice cubes

Method

Cut the tomatoes into chunks and place in a smoothie machine or blender with the green tea. Discard the skin and seeds from the watermelon, cut into chunks, and add to the tomatoes, together with the thyme, chive leaves, and ice cubes. If using a smoothie machine, blend on mix for 15 seconds and then on smooth for 45 seconds. In a blender, blend for 1–2 minutes until smooth. Pour into the glass, decorate, and serve.

Choose plump, ripe, and preferably organic tomatoes when making this drink, which is ideal for any time of the day. Thyme is good for counteracting excess sweating problems. Green tea helps in clearing up infections and improves the immune system, as well as helping the fight against heart disease and cancer.

ALTERNATIVE Other melons can be used in place of the watermelon—try galia or honeydew—and add an additional ⅔ cup freshly brewed green tea as well.

Strawberry & Rosemary Smoothie

SERVES 2

Ingredients

12 oz. ripe strawberries
1¼ cups organic bio live strawberry yogurt
1–2 fresh rosemary sprigs
4 ice cubes
mint sprigs, to decorate

Method

Lightly rinse the strawberries, reserve 1 or 2 for decorating and cut the remainder in half. Place in a smoothie machine or blender with the strawberry yogurt. Strip the leaves from the rosemary stalks and add the leaves with the ice cubes to the machine. If using a smoothie machine, blend on mix for 15 seconds and then on smooth for 45 seconds. In a blender, blend for 1–2 minutes until smooth. Pour into glasses, decorate, and serve.

Just because you are following a detox diet, there is no need for the food or drink you consume to be unpleasant. The addition of fresh rosemary with the strawberries in this recipe enhances the memory as well as improving the circulatory system.

ALTERNATIVE Try other fruits and flavored yogurts in place of the strawberries—raspberry, peach, or passion fruit with plain yogurt. If using passion fruit, strain the flesh and seeds before using if a smoother texture is preferred.

Peach & Passion Fruit Smoothie

SERVES 2

Ingredients

2 large, ripe peaches
2 ripe passion fruits
⅔ cup green tea
1¼ cups live plain yogurt
2 tbsp. rolled oats
few fresh basil leaves, plus extra to decorate
4 ice cubes

When buying peaches or nectarines, choose fruits that feel ripe when lightly pressed and have a good aroma. Fruits that are bought underripe often do not ripen properly and go woody. If your peaches do not appear to be ripening well, poach lightly in a little honey and water. In this recipe, the yogurt will help the digestive system and the rolled oats will help if following a glycemic index diet.

Method

Lightly rinse the peaches, cut in half, and discard the pits; reserve 2 slices for decoration. Place in a smoothie machine or blender. Scoop out the passion fruit pulp and seeds and strain if a smoother texture is preferred. Place in the machine together with the green tea, yogurt, rolled oats, basil, and ice cubes. If using a smoothie machine, blend on mix for 15 seconds and then on smooth for 45 seconds. In a blender, blend for 1–2 minutes until smooth. Pour into glasses, decorate, and serve.

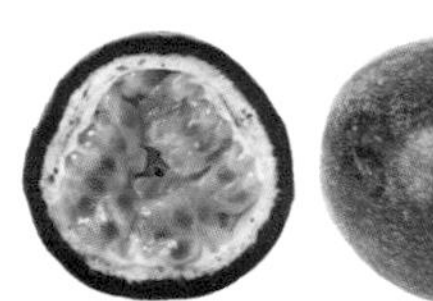

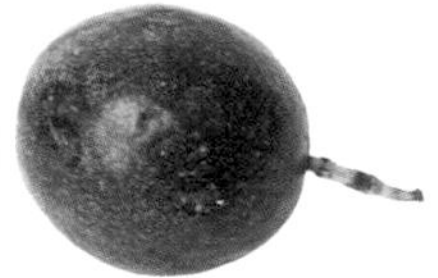

ALTERNATIVE If fresh peaches or nectarines are not available, try using plums, making sure that all the fruits are sound and not forgetting to discard the pits.

Blueberries with Aloe Vera & Yogurt

SERVES 1

Aloe vera is recognized as helping the body deal with constipation as well as many infections. The juice has a slightly bitter tang, so, by combining it with yogurt in this recipe, the bitterness is not apparent.

Ingredients

1 cup fresh blueberries
2 tbsp. aloe vera juice
4 tbsp. elderflower syrup
1¼ cups live plain yogurt
1 tbsp. flax oil
4 ice cubes
mint sprig, to decorate

Method

Lightly rinse the blueberries, reserve a few for decoration, and place the remainder in a smoothie machine or blender with the aloe vera juice, elderflower syrup, yogurt, flax oil, and ice cubes. If using a smoothie machine, blend on mix for 15 seconds and then on smooth for 45 seconds. In a blender, blend for 1–2 minutes until smooth. Pour into the glass, decorate, and serve.

ALTERNATIVE Add 1 cup raspberries to the blueberries and replace the plain yogurt with live raspberry yogurt.

Zucchini & Cucumber Smoothie

SERVES 2

Ingredients

1 whole English cucumber
1 medium zucchini
⅔ cup green tea
1¼ cups live plain yogurt
few fresh parsley sprigs, plus extra for decoration
2 fresh tarragon sprigs
4 ice cubes
8–10 whole chive leaves
extra chive leaves, or 2–4 chive flower heads, if available, to decorate

Method

Peel the cucumber, discard the seeds, and cut into chunks. Peel the zucchini and cut into chunks. Place all the ingredients, except the decoration, in a smoothie machine or blender. If using a smoothie machine, blend on mix for 15 seconds and then on smooth for 45 seconds. In a blender, blend for 1–2 minutes until smooth. Pour into glasses, decorate, and serve.

Serve this smoothie well chilled for maximum enjoyment—keeping the ingredients in the refrigerator and serving immediately will help. This smoothie is great for dealing with fluid retention.

ALTERNATIVE Other herbs that can be used in this recipe that help to relieve fluid retention include parsley, lovage, nettles, and dandelion.

Carrot with Apple & Sunflower Seeds

SERVES 2

All edible seeds are a good source of energy and minerals. Both are required when following a detox diet.

Ingredients

3 large carrots
1 large ripe apple
1¼ cups unsweetened apple juice
1 tbsp. sunflower seeds
8 ice cubes

Method

Peel the carrots and cut into chunks. Discard the core from the apple, reserve a slice for decoration, and cut the remainder into chunks. Place in a smoothie machine or blender with the remaining ingredients, including the ice cubes. If using a smoothie machine, blend on mix for 15 seconds and then on smooth for 45 seconds. In a blender, blend for 1–2 minutes until smooth. Pour into glasses, decorate, and serve.

ALTERNATIVE Use sesame seeds or flax seeds in place of the sunflower seeds, or try a combination of all three.

Beet & Apple Smoothie

SERVES 1

Ingredients

4 oz. beets
2 ripe apples
small piece fresh ginger
⅔ cup apple juice
1¼ cups live plain yogurt
few shakes cayenne pepper

Method

Cut the beets into chunks; core the apples and cut into chunks. Peel the ginger and chop. Place in a smoothie machine or blender together with the remaining ingredients. If using a smoothie machine, blend on mix for 15 seconds and then on smooth for 45 seconds. In a blender, blend for 1–2 minutes until smooth. Pour into the glass and serve.

Try this smoothie to help stimulate the lymphatic system. You can use either raw or cooked beets in this recipe. Obviously, using cooked beets is far easier than raw, but do ensure that you are using cooked beets that have not been steeped in vinegar, otherwise your smoothie will be very tart.

ALTERNATIVE Replace the live yogurt with either cranberry or orange juice.

Broccoli with Orange & Mint

SERVES 2

Broccoli is an excellent vegetable and provides a good source of fiber and antioxidants, which help in the fight against cancer. Mint is a great detox ingredient, while orange is full of vitamin C. Combined, they offer an extremely healthy and delicious detox drink.

Ingredients

3 cups broccoli florets
⅔ cup unsweetened orange juice
2 large oranges
2–3 fresh mint sprigs
1 tsp. flax seeds
4 ice cubes

Method

Cut the broccoli into small florets and place in a smoothie machine or blender with the orange juice. Cut a slice from 1 of the oranges and reserve for decoration. Peel the remaining oranges, discarding the bitter white pith, and divide into segments. Place in the machine with the remaining ingredients. If using a smoothie machine, blend on mix for 15 seconds and then on smooth for 45 seconds. In a blender, blend for 1–2 minutes until smooth. Pour the juice into glasses, decorate, and serve.

ALTERNATIVE Omit the fresh oranges and increase the amount of unsweetened orange juice to 1¼ cups. The smoothie will be thinner and more juicelike if not using fresh oranges.

Tomato, Apple & Basil Smoothie

SERVES 1

This recipe is great when following a detox regime and, provided you use unsweetened apple juice, it will not matter if you use whole apples or juice—both work very well.

Ingredients

2 medium, ripe tomatoes
1 apple
2 tsp. finely grated orange zest
4 tbsp. orange juice
few fresh basil sprigs, plus extra, to decorate
4 icc cubes

Method

Cut the tomatoes into chunks and place in a smoothie machine or blender with all the remaining ingredients. If using a smoothie machine, blend on mix for 15 seconds and then on smooth for 45 seconds. In a blender, blend for 1–2 minutes until smooth. Pour into the glass, decorate, and serve.

ALTERNATIVE For a speedier drink, replace the fresh tomatoes with 14 oz. canned chopped tomatoes, then add a few shakes cayenne pepper before blending with the other ingredients.

Tomato & Bell Pepper Smoothie

SERVES 1–2

Ingredients

2 medium, ripe tomatoes
⅓ cup freshly brewed green tea
1 large red bell pepper, skinned, if preferred
1 small shallot
few basil sprigs
6 ice cubes
cherry tomato and extra basil leaves, to decorate

Method

Cut the tomatoes into chunks and place in a smoothie machine or blender together with the green tea. Discard the seeds from the bell pepper, cut into chunks, and add to the tomatoes. Peel the shallot, chop, and add to the machine, together with the remaining ingredients. If using a smoothie machine, blend on mix for 15 seconds and then on smooth for 45 seconds. In a blender, blend for 1–2 minutes until smooth. Pour into glasses, decorate, and serve.

Try this smoothie with skinned bell peppers if time permits. Skinning bell peppers is easy—simply cut into quarters, discard the seeds, and put skin-side uppermost under a preheated broiler. Cook for 10 minutes, or until the skins begin to blacken. Let cool, then peel them off.

ALTERNATIVE The shallot will give this smoothie a very distinct onion taste—if preferred, replace with chive leaves, which, like shallots and onion, will also help combat fluid retention.

Zucchini with Avocado & Chile

SERVES 2

Ingredients

1 zucchini
2 ripe avocados
4 tbsp. lime juice
1¼ cups orange juice
1 chile, seeds discarded
4 ice cubes
2 tbsp. sour cream or live plain yogurt, to serve
2 lime slices, to decorate

Method

Peel the zucchini, discard the seeds, and cut into chunks. Cut the avocados in half, peel, and discard the pits. Place the zucchini avocado chunks, lime and orange juices, chile, and ice in a smoothie machine or blender. If using a smoothie machine, blend on mix for 15 seconds and then on smooth for 45 seconds. In a blender, blend for 1–2 minutes until smooth. Pour into glasses, top with a spoonful of sour cream or yogurt, decorate, and serve.

Avocados can only be bought fresh. Choose plump, undamaged fruits. Allow to ripen in the fruit bowl (not the refrigerator) and, once cut, use immediately. Avocado contains vitamin E as well as other vitamins and minerals that play a good part in reviving the system.

ALTERNATIVE Replace the lime juice with all orange juice for a slightly sweeter drink.

Creole Smoothie

SERVES 2

Ingredients

4 tbsp. lime juice
1¼ cups orange juice
3 medium carrots, peeled and chopped
⅓ cup trimmed and chopped okra
2 medium tomatoes, chopped
4 scallions, trimmed and chopped
1 tbsp. rolled oats
4 ice cubes
basil leaves, trimmed scallions and tomatoes, to decorate (optional)
2 cleaned and trimmed celery stalks with leaves still attached, for stirring (optional)

Method

Place all the ingredients to be blended in a smoothie machine or blender. If using a smoothie machine, blend on mix for 15 seconds and then on smooth for 45 seconds. In a blender, blend for 1–2 minutes until smooth. Pour into glasses, decorate, and serve immediately.

Unfortunately, this will have to be a seasonal drink, unless you live in an area where okra is readily available. Okra is full of soluble fiber, which not only helps in controlling blood cholesterol levels, but will also give a big energy boost.

ALTERNATIVE Add 1 seeded and chopped chile before blending or use a few dashes Tabasco sauce to spice it up and jump-start your day.

Sweet Potato with Apple & Chives

SERVES 1–2

Ingredients

2 medium sweet potatoes
2 celery stalks, trimmed
1¼ cups unsweetened apple juice
small handful fresh chives, plus 1–2 tsp. snipped chives, to decorate
6 ice cubes

Method

Peel the sweet potatoes and cut into chunks. Chop the celery, then place both vegetables into a smoothie machine or blender. Add the apple juice and chives with the ice cubes. If using a smoothie machine, blend on mix for 15 seconds and then on smooth for 45 seconds. In a blender, blend for 1–2 minutes until smooth. Pour into glasses, decorate, and serve.

Sweet potatoes are slightly overlooked by many people, which is a great shame. The sweet orange flesh combines well with many different flavors and, if following a glycemic index diet or just needing a quick pick-me-up, it is an excellent addition to the weekly shopping list.

ALTERNATIVE Yams could be used in place of the sweet potatoes and 2 ripe apples with mineral water in place of the apple juice.

Minty Pea & Cucumber Smoothie

SERVES 2

Ingredients

3½ cups sugar snap peas
1 English cucumber, peeled and cut into chunks
2 celery stalks, chopped
4 scallions, trimmed and chopped
⅔ cup low-fat milk
handful fresh mint
4 ice cubes
chilled mineral water, to dilute
2–3 tbsp. live plain yogurt, to serve
2 cucumber slices and mint sprigs, to decorate

Method

Place all the ingredients except the mineral water and yogurt in a smoothie machine or blender. If using a smoothie machine, blend on mix for 15 seconds and then on smooth for 45 seconds. In a blender, blend for 1–2 minutes until smooth. Pour into glasses, dilute if preferred, stir in the yogurt, decorate, and serve.

You can choose how you drink this—either as a deliciously different drink, or a cold, refreshing soup in the summer. Whichever way you choose, it is guaranteed to be very popular.

ALTERNATIVE Use snow peas in place of the sugar snap peas and replace the yogurt with a little light cream.

Fig, Coconut & Banana Smoothie

SERVES 1–2

Ingredients

½ cup ready-to-eat dried figs, chopped
2 ripe bananas
1¼ cups coconut milk
4 ice cubes

Method

Place the chopped figs into a smoothie machine or blender. Peel and cut the bananas into chunks and add to the machine with the coconut milk and ice cubes. If using a smoothie machine, blend on mix for 15 seconds and then on smooth for 45 seconds. In a blender, blend for 1–2 minutes until smooth. Pour into glasses and serve.

For maximum fiber content, use either dried fruits that need soaking and then poaching gently for about 10–15 minutes, or use ready-to-eat dried fruits, which do not need soaking first.

ALTERNATIVE Replace the bananas with the flesh from 2 ripe mangoes and simply place all the ingredients into the machine and blend.

Melon with Black Currant & Ginger

SERVES 1–2

Ingredients

½ galia melon
1¼ cups black currant juice or syrup
small piece fresh ginger
1–2 tsp. honey (optional)
2 pinches wheatgrass powder
4 ice cubes
mint sprigs, to decorate

Wheatgrass is one of the latest herbs to hit our shelves and has many properties. Among other things, it is an antioxidant and a great booster for the immune system. It comes from wheat grain that is allowed to sprout until it becomes young grass. It is then harvested and ground to form a powder.

Method

Remove the skin and seeds from the melon and cut into chunks. Place in a smoothie machine or blender with the black currant juice. Peel the ginger, chop, and add to the machine with the honey, if using, the wheatgrass powder, and the ice cubes. If using a smoothie machine, blend on mix for 15 seconds and then on smooth for 45 seconds. In a blender, blend for 1–2 minutes until smooth. Pour into glasses, decorate, and serve.

ALTERNATIVE Replace the 1¼ cups black currant juice with the same amount of orange juice.

Pear & Black Currant Mix

SERVES 1–2

This drink is quick and easy to make, ready in seconds, and guaranteed to refresh instantly.

Ingredients

1 medium parsnip, peeled
2 ripe pears, such as Conference, cored
1 cup black currant juice or cordial
4 ice cubes
mint sprigs, to decorate

Method

Cut the parsnip and pears into chunks, reserving 1 or 2 pear slices for decoration. Place the pear and parsnip chunks in a smoothie machine or blender with the black currant juice and ice cubes. If using a smoothie machine, blend on mix for 15 seconds and then on smooth for 45 seconds. In a blender, blend for 1–2 minutes until smooth. Pour into glasses, decorate, and serve immediately.

ALTERNATIVE Use plump, ripe black currants in place of the juice and swirl with a little live plain yogurt.

Red Cabbage with Celery & Carrot

SERVES 1–2

Ingredients

¼ small head red cabbage
3 celery stalks, trimmed
1 small carrot, peeled
2 tbsp. rolled oats
1¼ cups orange juice
4 ice cubes
blood orange slice, if available, to decorate

Method

Cut the cabbage into chunks, discarding the tough central stalk and the outer leaves. Cut the celery and carrot into chunks and place all the vegetables into a smoothie machine or blender. Add the oats with the orange juice and ice cubes. If using a smoothie machine, blend on mix for 15 seconds and then on smooth for 45 seconds. In a blender, blend for 1–2 minutes until smooth. Pour into glasses, decorate, and serve.

Red cabbage is more readily available in the winter months than the summer. When using, it is advisable to wash thoroughly in plenty of cold water and continue until the water runs clear. Discard any damaged or outside leaves.

ALTERNATIVE Replace the red cabbage with white cabbage and use unsweetened apple juice instead of orange.

Dates with Sweet Potato & Tomatoes

SERVES 2

Use fresh dates if available—although their carbohydrate content is not as high as dried, they are complemented by the addition of the sweet potatoes.

Ingredients

⅔ cup fresh or dried dates
1 large sweet potato, peeled
1 large, ripe tomato
1¼ cups orange juice
small handful fresh cilantro
8 ice cubes
cilantro sprigs and cherry tomatoes, to decorate

Method

Cut the dates in half and discard the pits. Cut the sweet potato and tomatoes into chunks and place in a smoothie machine or blender with the dates. Add the orange juice with the cilantro and ice cubes. If using a smoothie machine, blend on mix for 15 seconds and then on smooth for 45 seconds. In a blender, blend for 1–2 minutes until smooth. Pour into glasses, decorate, and serve.

ALTERNATIVE The dates can be replaced with dried or fresh apricots, or use a combination of both.

Melon & Elderflower Reviver

SERVES 1–2

Elderflower has a very delicate flavor and combines well with fruits, such as melon, apple, lemon, or lime.

Ingredients

½ ripe galia melon
⅓ cup elderflower syrup
4 ice cubes
iced sparkling water, to serve
1–2 lemon slices, to decorate

Method

Discard the skin and seeds from the melon, cut into chunks, and place in a smoothie machine or blender. Add the elderflower syrup and ice cubes. If using a smoothie machine, blend on mix for 15 seconds and then on smooth for 45 seconds. In a blender, blend for 1–2 minutes until smooth. Pour into glasses and fill up with the iced sparkling water. Decorate the glasses with a lemon slice and serve.

ALTERNATIVE Try using 2 peeled oranges or 2 cored apples in place of the melon.

Grapefruit Refresher

SERVES 2

Ingredients

1 red grapefruit
1 pink grapefruit
1 yellow grapefruit
1¼ cups orange juice
1–2 pinches blue-grass algae powder
8 ice cubes
sparkling water, to dilute
2 each lime slices and maraschino cherries, to decorate

Method

Peel all the grapefruits and divide into segments. Place in a smoothie machine or blender with the orange juice, blue-grass algae, and ice cubes. If using a smoothie machine, blend on mix for 15 seconds and then on smooth for 45 seconds. In a blender, blend for 1–2 minutes until smooth. Pour into glasses, dilute with water to taste, decorate, and serve.

It is now possible to buy three different colors of grapefruit: red, pink, and the traditional yellow variety. The red and pink are sweeter than the yellow and, by using all three, you will create a refreshing and stimulating drink which should not need any extra sweetness.

ALTERNATIVE Oranges can be used in place of the yellow grapefruit to provide a slightly sweeter drink. Replace the orange juice with grapefruit to give it a little more kick. A little honey could be added as well, if liked.

Breakfast Delight

SERVES 2

Ingredients

2 pink grapefruits
1 large orange
1 ripe papaya
1¼ cups red grapefruit juice
1–2 tbsp. muesli
pinch kelp powder
8 ice cubes
sparkling mineral water, to dilute
mint sprigs, to decorate

Method

Peel the grapefruits and orange and divide into segments. Peel the papaya, discard the seeds, and cut into chunks, reserving some for decoration. Place all the fruits with the juice, muesli, kelp powder, and ice cubes in a smoothie machine or blender. If using a smoothie machine, blend on mix for 15 seconds and then on smooth for 45 seconds. In a blender, blend for 1–2 minutes until smooth. Pour into glasses, top off with sparkling water, decorate, and serve.

Give your system a jump-start with this delicious drink—guaranteed to get you going and keep you going until lunchtime.

ALTERNATIVE Replace the muesli with a sugar-free homemade version—rolled oats, a few dried fruits, such as raisins, and a few toasted, slivered almonds.

Fig & Orange Smoothie

SERVES 1–2

Ingredients

4–6 fresh, ripe figs, depending on size, or ½ cup chopped ready-to-eat dried figs
⅔ cup mixed orange and apple juice
2 large oranges
1 ripe passion fruit
1–2 pinches spirulina powder
4 ice cubes
chilled mineral water, to dilute
orange wedges, to decorate

Method

Place the figs and fruit juice in a smoothie machine or blender. Peel the oranges, divide into segments, and add to the machine. Scoop the flesh and seeds from the passion fruit and add to the machine with the spirulina powder and ice. If using a smoothie machine, blend on mix for 15 seconds and then on smooth for 45 seconds. In a blender, blend for 1–2 minutes until smooth. Pour into glasses, dilute to taste with the mineral water, decorate, and serve.

If using dried figs, look for the ready-to-eat dried figs, because they will blend more quickly than fresh figs. Here, the figs are combined with orange and passion fruit, creating an aromatic and refreshing drink.

ALTERNATIVE The figs can be replaced with ready-to-eat dried or fresh apricots. If using fresh, cut in half and discard the pits, then proceed as above.

Beet, Pear & Apple Reviver

SERVES 1

This great recipe is packed full of energy-giving produce that will help to revive you and keep you going throughout the day.

Ingredients

4 oz. cooked beet
1 apple, such as Granny Smith
1 large, ripe pear, such as Conference
2–3 tsp. honey
1 cup apple juice

Method

Cut the beet into chunks and place in a smoothie machine or blender. Peel the apple and pear, discard the cores, and cut into slices, reserving one for decoration. Add the remainder to the machine, together with the honey and apple juice. If using a smoothie machine, blend on mix for 15 seconds and then on smooth for 45 seconds. In a blender, blend for 1–2 minutes until smooth. Pour into the glass, decorate, and serve.

ALTERNATIVE Replace the apples with oranges and use orange juice instead of the apple juice.

Red & Green Mix

SERVES 1–2

Here, red and green grapes are used with plump, lush cherries, which are bursting with flavor. Cherries have a limited season, so take advantage of them when around and enjoy this fabulous pick-me-up.

Ingredients

¾ cup seedless red grapes
¾ cup seedless green grapes
1 cup cherries
⅔ cup freshly brewed ginseng tea
4 ice cubes, to serve

Method

Rinse the grapes and reserve a few for decoration. Remove any stalks and then place in a smoothie machine or blender. Pit the cherries and add to the grapes together with the ginseng tea. If using a smoothie machine, blend on mix for 15 seconds and then on smooth for 45 seconds. In a blender, blend for 1–2 minutes until smooth. Place the ice cubes into glasses, add the smoothie, decorate, and serve.

ALTERNATIVE For a more indulgent drink, top each filled glass with a spoonful of live cherry-flavored yogurt and sprinkle with a little grated chocolate.

Orange with Wheatgrass & Yogurt

SERVES 1–2

Ingredients

1 large orange
juice of 1 lemon
⅔ cup orange or mandarin juice
1 tsp. honey (optional)
1 pinch wheatgrass powder
⅔ cup live plain yogurt
4 ice cubes
lemon slice(s), to decorate

Method

Peel the orange and divide into segments. Place in a smoothie machine or blender along with the fruit juices, honey if using, and the wheatgrass powder. If using a smoothie machine, blend on mix for 15 seconds and then on smooth for 45 seconds. In a blender, blend for 1–2 minutes. Add the yogurt and ice cubes and blend for another 20–40 seconds in a smoothie machine or another minute in a blender until smooth. Pour into glasses, decorate, and serve.

Wheatgrass can be used in the diet for a variety of reasons. It acts as a natural tonic to the system as well as being good for detoxification. Here, it is combined with oranges and is perfect for an early morning start.

ALTERNATIVE Replace the orange with 1 pink grapefruit and, if a slightly sweeter drink is preferred, add a little extra honey. Do taste first before adding more honey.

Pomelo & Mandarin Smoothie

SERVES 1

Ingredients

1 pomelo
3 mandarins
⅔ cup freshly brewed green tea
2 tbsp. muesli
1 pinch blue-grass algae powder
4 ice cubes
mint sprig, to decorate

Method

Peel the pomelo, discarding the bitter white pith, and divide into segments. Peel the mandarins, reserving 1 wedge for decoration, and discard any seeds. Place both fruits in a smoothie machine or blender, along with the green tea, muesli, blue-grass algae, and ice cubes. If using a smoothie machine, blend on mix for 15 seconds and then on smooth for 45 seconds. In a blender, blend for 1–2 minutes until smooth. Pour into the glass, decorate, and serve.

Pomelos are the largest of the citrus fruits and have a thick, pale green skin. The flesh is similar to grapefruit, slightly more tart, and often in need of a little extra sweetness. Combined with mandarins—small fruits with an easy-to-peel skin and sweet flesh—the flavors balance each other out.

ALTERNATIVE Use other fruits in place of the pomelo, if liked; try a mixture of pink, red and yellow grapefruit or 1 medium, ripe pineapple.

Kiwis with Blueberries

SERVES 1

Ingredients

4 kiwis
⅔ cup live plain yogurt
1 cup blueberries
1 tbsp. flax oil
4 ice cubes
kiwi wedge and a few blueberries, to decorate

Method

Scoop the flesh from each kiwi and place in a smoothie machine or blender along with the remaining ingredients, including the ice cubes. If using a smoothie machine, blend on mix for 15 seconds and then on smooth for 45 seconds. In a blender, blend for 1–2 minutes until smooth. Pour into the glass, decorate, and serve.

Kiwis contain high levels of vitamin C and provide a refreshing, instant pick-me-up when blended into a drink.

ALTERNATIVE The blueberries can be replaced with raspberries or strawberries, if liked.

Nonalcoholic Cocktails

Virgin Mary

SERVES 1

Ingredients

4 ice cubes
5 measures tomato juice
½ –1 tsp.Tabasco sauce
1–2 dashes Worcestershire sauce
1 tsp. freshly squeezed lemon juice
celery stalk and lemon twist, to decorate

Known affectionately as a "Bloody Shame" due to its lack of alcohol, the Virgin Mary is derived from the alcoholic cocktail the Bloody Mary (*see* page 178). Theories about the origins of the more famous "Bloody Mary" name are abundant. From stories about a Chicago bar called the Bucket of Blood to claims of royal inspiration from Mary, Queen of Scots, the etymology of the cocktail is quite varied.

One of the more plausible claims to the Bloody Mary recipe and name came from an American bartender working in Harry's New York Bar in Paris during the 1920s. He originally concocted the drink with equal parts vodka and tomato juice, but later added lemon, pepper, Tabasco sauce, and Worcestershire sauce when he returned to the United States. It is also noted that the bartender acknowledged the suggestion for the name came from a patron recalling the Bucket of Blood bar in Chicago.

Method

Place the ice cubes into a glass and pour over the tomato juice. Add the Tabasco sauce to taste, together with the Worcestershire sauce and lemon juice. Stir well until mixed, then serve decorated with the celery stalk and lemon twist.

ALTERNATIVE If liked, make this a tall drink. Fill a tall glass halfway with crushed ice and pour in the tomato juice. Add the Tabasco and Worcestershire sauces to taste, together with the lemon juice and top off with club soda. Use the celery stalk as the

Spicy Mary

SERVES 2

Ingredients

2 medium ripe tomatoes, chopped
2 tsp. freshly snipped chives
2 tsp. freshly chopped cilantro
1 tsp. finely grated lemon zest
½ small jalapeño chile, seeded
few shakes Worcestershire sauce
4–6 ice cubes
6 measures ginger beer
celery stalks, for stirring (optional)

Method

Place all the ingredients except the ice cubes, ginger beer, and celery stalks in a smoothie machine or blender. If using a smoothie machine, blend on mix for 15 seconds and then on smooth for 45 seconds. If using a blender, blend for 1–2 minutes until smooth. Place the ice cubes in glasses, fill halfway with the Spicy Mary, and top off with ginger beer. Serve with a celery stalk to use as a stirrer.

If liked, you could frost the rim of the glasses for this recipe. Place some salt in a saucer to a depth of ¼ inch. Rub the rim of the glass with a little lemon or lime juice, then dip in the salt, letting it set before using.

ALTERNATIVE Replace the ginger beer with vodka and wait for the buzz!

Strawberry Kiss

SERVES 1

If the strawberries that you are using are not that ripe, slice and sprinkle with either a little freshly ground black pepper or balsamic vinegar. Let stand for 1–2 hours, then use as directed. The strawberries can also be heated briefly in a microwave; this will help the flavor immensely.

Ingredients

3 measures strawberry puree
1½ measures freshly squeezed orange juice
1 measure freshly squeezed lemon juice
3 ice cubes, crushed
3–4 measures lemon-flavor soda
1 tbsp. whipped cream
freshly grated chocolate
1 strawberry slice, to decorate

Method

Place the strawberry puree in a cocktail shaker or pitcher and add the orange and lemon juices. Shake for 20 seconds, or until blended. If using a pitcher, stir vigorously until thoroughly blended. Place the crushed ice in a glass and pour over the strawberry mixture. Top off with the soda and float the whipped cream on top. Sprinkle the cream with the chocolate and decorate with a strawberry slice. Serve with a straw.

ALTERNATIVE Try using other flavor fruit purees; try raspberry, a mixture of berries, mango, or papaya.

Hawaiian Island Surfer

SERVES 1

Ingredients

2 measures tropical fruit juice
1 measure cream of coconut
3 scoops lemon sorbet (or water ice)
4 measures ginger ale
papaya and pineapple wedges and maraschino cherry, to decorate

Method

Place the tropical fruit juice into a chilled glass or flute and stir in the cream of coconut. Add scoops of lemon sorbet (or water ice) and top off with the ginger ale. Thread the fruits on a toothpick to decorate and place across the glass. Serve.

Part of the pleasure of a drink, especially at a party, is its look. The decoration should reflect the flavors of the drink itself. Here, the tropical feel is echoed in the use of wedges of papaya and pineapple.

ALTERNATIVE Use pineapple juice instead of "tropical" juice, if preferred.

Virgin Raspberry Daiquiri

SERVES 1

Ingredients

1 tsp. superfine sugar
3 measures raspberry syrup or fresh fruit puree
2 measures pineapple juice
½ measure lemon juice
4 ice cubes, crushed
lemon-flavor soda
fresh raspberries threaded onto a toothpick and mint sprig, to decorate

Method

Place the superfine sugar into a saucer and place some water in another saucer. Dip the rim of a chilled glass into the water and then into the sugar. Turn the rim until well coated in the sugar, then chill until required. Pour the raspberry syrup or fresh fruit puree into a cocktail shaker or pitcher and add the pineapple and lemon juices. Shake or stir until well blended. Place the crushed ice into the sugared glass and pour over the blended drink. Top off with the soda, decorate, and serve.

Alcohol-free cocktails are the perfect answer for underage teenagers. Serve a selection to them, beautifully decorated with straws, umbrellas, and pieces of fruit and wow them all.

ALTERNATIVE Replace the raspberry syrup with cranberry juice and the pineapple juice with mango juice.

Southern Ginger

SERVES 1

This tangy drink is perfect for hot sunny days and will certainly help to keep the temperature down. It is a good idea to chill the lemon-flavor soda beforehand and, once it is opened, remember to keep the bottle tightly screwed down to keep the fizz in.

Ingredients

- 5 measures dry ginger ale, plus extra to top off
- 1 measure freshly squeezed lemon juice
- ½ –1 tsp. sugar syrup (*see* page 31)
- 3 ice cubes, crushed
- mint sprig, to decorate

Method

Place the dry ginger ale into an old-fashioned glass and stir in the lemon juice and sugar syrup to taste. Spoon in the crushed ice and top off with more ginger ale. Decorate with a mint sprig and serve with a stirrer and a straw.

ALTERNATIVE If liked, use ginger beer and make into a short drink by halving the amount of ginger beer and pouring into a short glass over ice cubes. Add lemon-flavor soda, if liked, or use ginger ale instead.

Acapulco Gold

SERVES 1

Ingredients

4 ice cubes, crushed
3 measures pineapple juice
1 measure grapefruit juice
1 measure cream of coconut
3–4 measures lemon-flavor soda
1 tbsp. whipped cream
few dry coconut flakes and mint sprig, to decorate

Method

Place the crushed ice into a cocktail shaker and pour in the pineapple and grapefruit juices. Add the cream of coconut and shake for 20 seconds, or until well blended. Strain into a chilled glass and top off with the soda. Float the whipped cream on top and serve decorated with the dry coconut flakes and mint sprig.

If you have a fresh coconut, it is very easy to make your own coconut flakes. Simply break the fruit in half, reserving the coconut juice inside to add to the drink. Using a swivel vegetable peeler, simply cut off very thin flakes of the fresh coconut. These can be lightly dried out in a warm oven and this will keep the flakes for longer. Remember to store in an airtight container. Fresh flakes should be used within 2–3 days.

ALTERNATIVE Try apple juice instead of pineapple juice, if preferred.

Apple of My Eye

SERVES 1

Ingredients

3 ice cubes
3 measures clear apple juice
1½ measures black currant syrup
lemon-flavor soda
1 scoop good-quality vanilla ice cream
red apple wedge and mint sprig, to decorate

Method

Place the ice in a cocktail shaker and pour in the apple juice and black currant syrup. Shake until blended, then strain into a tall glass. Top off with the soda and place the scoop of ice cream on top. Decorate with the apple wedge and mint sprig.

Black currants can be difficult to find because they are banned in some states, and where they do grow, they are available only seasonally. If you find fresh black currants in your area, buy some and freeze them so that you have them whenever you want.

ALTERNATIVE Try blending 1 measure whipped cream with the ingredients instead of floating ice cream on top.

Bora Bora

SERVES 1

Ingredients

3 measures pineapple juice
3 measures ginger beer
1 measure cream of coconut
1 measure grenadine
½ tsp. ground ginger
1 measure freshly squeezed lime juice
1–2 tsp. ginger syrup (use the syrup from a jar of preserved ginger)
4 ice cubes, crushed
lime wedges, to decorate

Method

Pour the pineapple juice, the ginger beer, cream of coconut, and grenadine, together with the ground ginger, to taste, the freshly squeezed lime juice, and the preserved ginger syrup; into a cocktail shaker. Shake for 20 seconds, or until well blended. Place the crushed ice into an old-fashioned glass and pour in the cocktail. Decorate with the lime wedges.

Bora Bora is a Tahitian island that is surrounded by a lagoon and fringing reef. The center of the island is dominated by the remnants of an extinct volcano, which has two distinct peaks. The word actually means "peace," which is reflected in the delicious drink below.

ALTERNATIVE Top with an extra spoonful of cream of coconut and decorate with shavings of fresh coconut.

Brontosaurus

SERVES 1

Ingredients

3 measures red grapefruit juice
2 measures freshly squeezed orange juice
1 measure freshly squeezed lemon juice
1 measure freshly squeezed lime juice
½ measure grenadine
4 ice cubes, crushed
2–3 dashes Worcestershire sauce
orange and lemon twists, plus lime slice, to decorate

Method

Place all the fruit juices into a cocktail shaker with the grenadine and crushed ice. Shake until blended, then pour into a glass and add Worcestershire sauce to taste. Serve decorated with the fruit twists.

The name of the drink actually means "thunder lizard" in Greek and refers back to when dinosaurs ruled the world. This drink, however, is bang up to date and in the twenty-first century. Perfect any time, day or evening.

ALTERNATIVE Replace the grapefruit with carrot juice and add a few dashes of Tabasco sauce to taste. Season with a little freshly ground black pepper and serve with a celery stalk as a stirrer.

Mickey Mouse

SERVES 1

Ingredients

3 ice cubes
5 measures chilled cola
1 scoop good-quality vanilla ice cream
1 scoop good-quality chocolate ice cream
1 tbsp. whipped cream
½ tsp. finely grated chocolate
1 maraschino cherry, to decorate

Method

Place the ice cubes into a tall glass and pour in the chilled cola. Top with the scoops of vanilla and chocolate ice cream and the whipped cream and sprinkle with the grated chocolate. Decorate with the cherry and serve with a spoon.

As with the character Mickey Mouse, this drink is loved by all the "young at heart." Crammed full of delicious ice cream floating on top of chilled cola, what could be better on a hot day to keep the temperature down?

ALTERNATIVE Place a few fresh strawberries and raspberries on top of crushed ice. Add the cola and then the ice cream and serve sprinkled with the grated chocolate.

Canadian Pride

SERVES 1

Ingredients

- 3 measures pink grapefruit juice
- 2 measures maple syrup
- 1½ –2 measures freshly squeezed lemon juice
- 1 measure ginger ale
- 4 ice cubes
- lemon zest twist, to decorate

Maple syrup is the flagship where food is concerned for Canada and is used extensively in both food and drinks. It is a sweetener that is made from the sap of the maple tree. It is produced in a sugarbush, or sugarwood—these are wooded shacks where the sap is boiled down to a syrup.

Method

Pour the grapefruit juice with the maple syrup and 1 measure of lemon juice into a cocktail shaker and shake for 30 seconds, or until blended. Check for sweetness and, if necessary, add the remaining lemon juice and shake again. Add the ginger ale and shake briefly. Place the ice into a glass and pour over the drink. Decorate with the lemon zest twist and serve.

ALTERNATIVE Try decorating with a slice of grapefruit instead of lemon zest.

Passion Cooler

SERVES 1

It is best when using passion fruits to buy at least 4 days before you want to use them. Let ripen in the fruit bowl instead of keeping in the refrigerator. It is a matter of personal preference as to whether you use the seeds.

Ingredients

2 measures freshly squeezed orange juice
2 measures mango juice
1 measure pineapple juice
1 ripe passion fruit
½ ripe banana, mashed
4 ice cubes, crushed
orange, lime and pineapple wedges, to decorate

Method

Pour the orange, mango, and pineapple juices into a cocktail shaker. Scoop out the seeds and pulp from the passion fruit and place in the cocktail shaker together with the banana. Shake for 30 seconds, or until well blended. Place the crushed ice into a tall glass and pour over the blended juice. Thread the fruit wedges onto a toothpick and place across the glass to decorate.

ALTERNATIVE Replace the passion fruit with 1–2 teaspoons grenadine.

Queen Charlie

SERVES 1

If you want to use a fresh mango to provide the juice for this drink, do make sure that the fruit is ripe and unblemished. Peel, discarding the pit, then blend in a liquidizer or food processor.

Ingredients

1 measure grenadine
1 measure guava juice
1 measure mango juice
3 ice cubes
lemon-flavor soda
maraschino cherry, to decorate

Method

Pour the grenadine into a cocktail shaker together with the guava and mango juices. Add the ice and shake for 30 seconds, or until blended. Pour into an old-fashioned glass and top off with soda. Thread the cherry on a toothpick and use to decorate the glass.

ALTERNATIVE Use other tropical fruit juices according to personal preference and add a mashed banana to make a thicker drink.

Pomola

SERVES 1

A pomelo is the largest of the citrus fruits and has a very thick green skin with thick white pith. The flesh is very fibrous and can be bitter, so be prepared to add a little more sweetness.

Ingredients

3 ice cubes
2 measures pomelo juice
½ measure grenadine
2–3 tsp., or to taste, syrup from a jar of maraschino cherries
5 measures chilled cola
maraschino cherry and lime wedge, to decorate

Method

Place the ice cubes in a tall glass and pour in the pomelo juice. Add the grenadine and maraschino cherry syrup and stir well. Top off with the chilled cola and serve decorated with the maraschino cherry and lime wedge.

ALTERNATIVE Replace the pomelo juice with grapefruit juice; use yellow, pink, or red grapefruit. The pink and red grapefruits are slightly sweeter than the yellow variety.

Magnificent Peach

SERVES 1

Ingredients

2 ripe peaches, pitted
1 measure orange juice
1–2 drops almond extract
3 ice cubes
chilled lemon-flavor soda
1 scoop raspberry sorbet
peach and fresh raspberries, to decorate

Method

Slice the peaches and place in a blender or smoothie machine with the orange juice and almond extract. Blend until smooth, then strain into a glass. Add the ice, then pour in the chilled soda and top off with a scoop of raspberry sorbet. Place a long-handled spoon into the glass, decorate, and serve.

This delicious drink is a luscious fruit salad in a glass and is perfect for hot summer days or evenings. Suitable for all ages, it is very easy to vary this recipe by using different flavored fruit juices.

ALTERNATIVE The peach can be replaced with nectarines, either the white- or yellow-fleshed varieties. Use according to personal preference or availability, but do make sure they are ripe.

Tarzan's Juicy Cooler

SERVES 1

You may not be swinging through the trees after drinking this, but it will certainly keep you cool when the weather gets hot.

Ingredients

3 measures freshly squeezed orange juice
3 measures pineapple juice
½ measure lemon juice
2 oz. ripe strawberries, lightly rinsed
3 ice cubes
chilled sparkling water
1 scoop strawberry ice cream
mint sprig, to decorate

Method

Place all the fruit juices into a blender or liquidizer. Reserve 1 of the strawberries to decorate. Slice the remaining strawberries and place into the blender or liquidizer and blend for 30 seconds. Strain, then pour into a tall glass and add the ice cubes. Top off with the chilled sparkling water and float the strawberry ice cream on top. Decorate with the strawberry and mint sprig.

ALTERNATIVE Use fresh raspberries and raspberry ripple ice cream in place of the strawberries and strawberry ice cream.

Summer Rain

SERVES 1

Ingredients

1 measure freshly squeezed orange juice
1 measure freshly squeezed lemon juice
2 measures mango juice
½ cup fresh ripe raspberries, lightly rinsed
4 ice cubes
chilled lemon-flavor soda
1 scoop lemon sorbet (or water ice)

Method

Pour the fruit juices into a blender. Reserve 2–3 raspberries to decorate and add the remainder to the blender. Blend for 30 seconds, or until well blended, then strain. Place the ice cubes into a tall glass and pour over the strained drink. Top off with the soda and float the lemon sorbet on top. Decorate with the reserved raspberries and serve.

When using raspberries in a puree, it is always a good idea to strain the puree afterward to remove the seeds, which, if still present, can seriously affect the feel of the drink.

ALTERNATIVE Ice cream can replace the sorbet, if liked; try a scoop or two of chocolate ice cream and then sprinkle with a little grated chocolate—delicious, of course!

Fruit Flip

SERVES 1

Ingredients

1 medium orange, preferably organic
1 ripe lemon, preferably organic
1 medium organic egg
1–2 tsp., or to taste, superfine sugar
3 ice cubes
orange and lemon twists, to decorate

Method

Squeeze the juice from both the orange and the lemon. Whisk the egg with sugar to taste until creamy, then gradually whisk in the orange and lemon juices. Strain into an old-fashioned glass and top off with ice cubes. Decorate with the orange and lemon twists and serve.

It is always best when possible to use organic produce, because it is grown without the aid of artificial fertilizers or pesticides. It can be used with confidence and is guaranteed to be chemical free.

ALTERNATIVE Replace the lemon with the juice from 1 pink grapefruit. Decorate with a thin slice from the grapefruit and an orange slice.

Pine Lime Sparkle

SERVES 1

Ingredients

3 measures pineapple juice
1 measure freshly squeezed lime juice
2 measures freshly squeezed lemon juice
1–2 tsp., or to taste, confectioners' sugar
3 ice cubes
chilled lemon-flavor soda
1 small wedge pineapple, lemon and lime twists, to decorate

Method

Place the pineapple juice with the lime and lemon juices into a cocktail shaker and add 1 teaspoon sugar. Shake for 30 seconds, or until blended. Taste for sweetness and, if necessary, add the remaining sugar and shake again. Place the ice into a tall glass and pour in the blended juice. Top off with the soda and decorate with the pineapple wedge and lemon and lime twists.

It is recommended that, in order to maintain a healthy lifestyle, we should all eat at least five portions of fruits or vegetables a day. Fruit juice counts for the same as a piece of fruit. Here, you have the recommended daily dose in one glass.

ALTERNATIVE For a sweeter drink, replace either the lime or lemon juice with orange juice.

Summertime Cooler

SERVES 1

If you have a smoothie machine, it can be used for all the fruit-based drinks. It will blend the fruits to a good consistency and ensure that all the valuable fiber is included in the drink.

Ingredients

2 oz. ripe strawberries, lightly rinsed
½ cup raspberries, lightly rinsed
1 ripe plum, rinsed, pitted, and sliced
1 tsp. honey
3 ice cubes, crushed
5 measures chilled sparkling water
1 scoop good-quality ice cream
mint sprig, to decorate

Method

Place the fruits into a blender together with the honey and blend for 30 seconds. Rub through a strainer and pour into a glass. Add the ice cubes and top off with the chilled sparkling water. Place the scoop of ice cream on top and add a long-handled spoon to the glass. Serve decorated with a mint sprig.

ALTERNATIVE Replace the sparkling water with ginger ale or club soda. Use soda if a sweet drink is required.

Prohibition Punch

SERVES 10

Ingredients

1 red apple, rinsed
4–5 mint sprigs
8–10 ice cubes
3 measures sugar syrup (*see* page 31)
2½ cups clear apple juice
1¼ cups cranberry juice
1¼ cups cold, freshly brewed peppermint tea

Method

Core the apple and chop, then place in a large glass pitcher together with the mint sprigs and ice cubes. Pour in the sugar syrup, together with the apple and cranberry juices. Stir in the cold tea, stir well, and let stand for at least 20 minutes to let the flavors mingle. Serve in old-fashioned glasses, ensuring that each glass gets 1–2 pieces of apple.

Prohibition occurred in many countries in the early twentieth century, but it was most notorious in the United States, where it was illegal to sell, make, transport, or consume alcohol between 1920 and 1933. Russia, Iceland, Norway, and Finland also enforced prohibition laws around this period. This punch would have been ideal to serve then.

ALTERNATIVE Use black currant syrup in place of the apple juice and decorate the glasses with fresh black currant sprigs, if you grow your own.

Aromatic Cup

SERVES 10

The fragrant aroma of this cup is due to the addition of the star anise, cinnamon sticks, cardamom pods, and passion fruit.

Ingredients

2½ cups apple juice
1¼ cups freshly brewed green tea
finely peeled zest of 1 and juice of 2 ripe limes
6 cardamom pods, cracked
3 whole star anise
2 cinnamon sticks, bruised
½–1 small red chile, seeded
2 ripe passion fruits
10 ice cubes
1¼ cups sparkling water
⅔ cup chopped litchis
cinnamon sticks, to serve

Method

Pour the juice and tea into a saucepan. Add the lime zest and juice to the pan with the spices and the chile. Bring slowly to a boil, then remove from the heat. Scoop out the pulp and seeds from the passion fruits and add to the pan. Cover and let cool for at least 1 hour. Strain into a bowl. Add the ice, stir in the water and litchis, and serve.

ALTERNATIVE Add a little dark brown sugar when heating the apple juice. Do remember to remove the spices before serving.

Spicy Cooler

SERVES 10

Ingredients

2¼ cups orange juice
thinly pared zest and juice from 1 lemon, preferably organic
1¼ cups pineapple juice
1¼ cups freshly brewed tea
3–4 tbsp., or to taste, honey
small piece fresh ginger, peeled and grated
6 whole cloves
2 cinnamon sticks, lightly bruised
1 small orange, preferably organic
10–20 orange wedges, to serve

Method

Add all the ingredients except the small orange to a heavy saucepan. Heat gently until hot, but be careful to not let the liquid boil. Thinly slice the orange and cut into small wedges. Add to the saucepan and heat for another 10 minutes. Strain into a heatproof bowl. Serve either warm or cool, ensuring that each glass gets a wedge or two of orange.

The addition of spices to this punch infuses it with such incredible flavor that the alcohol is not missed at all. Try serving it to your friends and listen to all the praise they will heap on you.

ALTERNATIVE Use light brown sugar in place of the honey. Add 1–2 star anise and 3 cracked cardamom pods for a real taste of the East.

Barbary Ale

SERVES 10

Ingredients

4 large oranges, preferably organic
2 ripe lemons, preferably organic
2½ cups filtered or mineral water
½ cup light brown sugar
2 tsp. ground cinnamon
1½ tsp. ground allspice
2½ cups ginger beer
1 lemon, to decorate
10 ice cubes

In place of the brown sugar you can try a raw sugar, such as turbinado sugar—a coarse sugar with a molasses flavor.

Method

Thinly peel the rind from 1 of the oranges and squeeze the juice from all the fruit. Place the rind and juices into a heavy saucepan. Add the water and sugar. Spoon the cinnamon and allspice into a small bowl and blend to a smooth paste with 2 tablespoons water. Stir into the saucepan. Stir frequently over gentle heat until the sugar has completely dissolved. Continue to heat gently for 15–20 minutes, stirring occasionally, until hot. Remove from the heat and let cool for at least 1 hour before straining into a punch bowl. Stir in the ginger beer. Thinly slice the lemon and cut each slice into triangles. Add to the punch bowl with the ice cubes. Serve cold in old-fashioned glasses.

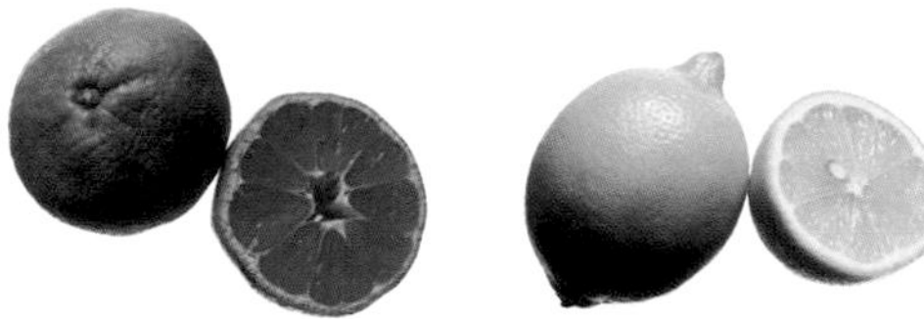

ALTERNATIVE If ginger beer is not your favorite, replace with ginger ale or another flavor of soda.

Apéritifs

Dry Martini

SERVES 1

Ingredients

4 ice cubes
½ measure dry vermouth
3 measures gin
1 green olive or lemon zest twist, to decorate

Perhaps the most famous cocktail of all thanks to Sean Connery when playing the suave, debonair James Bond as first immortalized in Ian Fleming's novels. This was his choice of cocktail, but he liked his "shaken, not stirred," with one exception—in *You Only Live Twice*, it is "stirred, not shaken"!

The origin of the cocktail, as with many, is not clear-cut. One story goes that it started life as the "Martinez," after the name of a Californian town. This was a much sweeter drink, using aromatic bitters, sweet red vermouth instead of dry white, sweeter Old Tom Gin, and a maraschino cherry instead of an olive. It is argued that, over time, the ingredients were changed one by one to the more typical combination we know today. Some say that the name came from the brand of vermouth most commonly used, made by Martini & Rossi. Here, both methods—shaken and stirred—are given. (*See* also page 205, the 007 Vodka Martini—James Bond was a fan of both.)

Method 1

Place the ice cubes into a cocktail shaker and add the vermouth and gin. Stir with a long-handled bar spoon, then strain into a chilled cocktail glass. Decorate with a green olive on a toothpick, or a lemon zest twist.

Method 2

Place the ice, vermouth, and gin in a cocktail shaker and shake vigorously for 1 minute. Pour into a frosted cocktail glass (*see* page 29) and decorate with an olive or a lemon twist.

ALTERNATIVE To turn this drink into a Buckeye Martini, simply decorate with a black olive instead of a green one.

Bloody Mary

SERVES 1

Ingredients

1 measure vodka
3 measures tomato juice
½ tsp. lemon juice
2 dashes Worcestershire sauce
3–4 dashes Tabasco sauce
pinch each of salt and freshly ground black pepper
celery stalk, as a stirrer
lemon slice, to decorate

Method

Place all the ingredients except the celery and decoration into a cocktail shaker and shake for 1 minute. Strain into an old-fashioned glass (*see* page 30), add the celery stalk to use as a stirrer and decorate with a lemon slice.

Reputed to have been devised in Harry's Bar, New York, in 1921, it became all the rage in 1931 once Prohibition had ended (*see* page 146 for more history on the Bloody Mary).

ALTERNATIVE Place some ice cubes, if liked, in the glass before pouring the cocktail over. Replace the vodka with gin—this is known as a Red Snapper.

Manhattan

SERVES 1

Ingredients

3–4 ice cubes, broken
2 measures rye whiskey or bourbon
1 measure sweet vermouth
4 drops Angostura bitters
1 maraschino cherry on a toothpick

Method

Place the broken ice into a cocktail shaker. Pour in the rye whiskey or bourbon with the sweet vermouth and add the Angostura bitters. Shake for 20 seconds, then pour unstrained into a cocktail glass and decorate with the cherry.

This cocktail takes its name from New York's most popular lunch area, which boasts some of the trendiest lunch restaurants in the city.

ALTERNATIVE Replace the rye whiskey or bourbon with brandy to serve a Brandy Manhattan.

Screwdriver

SERVES 1

Ingredients

4 ice cubes, crushed
2 measures vodka
4 measures freshly squeezed orange juice
1 small orange slice and 1 maraschino cherry, to decorate

Method

Place all the ingredients except the decoration into a chilled cocktail glass and stir with a bar spoon. Decorate with the orange slice and cherry, then serve.

There are a few theories as to the origins of the name of this famous cocktail. One is that an American oilman stationed in Iran was seen stirring his drink with his screwdriver.

ALTERNATIVE The vodka can be replaced with either rum or gin to create a Screwdriver Rum or Screwdriver Gin.

Rusty Nail

SERVES 1

Ingredients

2 ice cubes
1 measure Scotch whisky
½ measure Drambuie
lemon zest spiral, to decorate

Method

Place the ice cubes into an old-fashioned glass (*see* page 30) and pour over the whisky. Pour the Drambuie into the glass over the back of a bar spoon. Stir lightly with the bar spoon and serve decorated with the lemon zest spiral.

The whisky liqueur Drambuie has overtones of honey and heather and is reputed to date back to Bonnie Prince Charlie in Scotland.

ALTERNATIVE For a slightly sweeter taste, add a few squeezes of orange juice once the ice cubes have been placed in the glass, then proceed as above. Replace the lemon with an orange zest spiral.

Frozen Daiquiri

SERVES 1

Developed in Cuba around 1896, this very popular classic cocktail can be found on most bar menus. Try some of the other delicious variations that can be found.

Ingredients

4 ice cubes, crushed
freshly squeezed juice from 2 ripe limes
1 tsp. sugar syrup (*see* page 31)
2 measures white rum
lime wedge, to decorate

Method

Place the crushed ice into a cocktail shaker and pour in the lime juice, sugar syrup, and white rum. Shake for 1 minute, or until the shaker feels very cold. Strain into the chilled glass. Serve decorated with the lime wedge.

ALTERNATIVE Try a Melon Daiquiri by adding 2 measures Midori (melon liqueur) and use only 1 measure freshly squeezed lime juice.

Whisky Mac

SERVES 1

Ingredients

2–3 ice cubes, broken
1 measure Scotch whisky
1 measure ginger wine

Method

Fill an old-fashioned glass (*see* page 30) halfway with the broken ice and pour over the whisky. Add the ginger wine, stir, and serve.

The popularity of this drink is such that many people do not realize that it is in fact a cocktail. It is a great winter warmer that is enjoyed across the world.

ALTERNATIVE Ginger ale can be used in place of the ginger wine.

Brandy Sidecar

SERVES 1

This was created in Paris just after the Second World War. It was made especially for an army officer who arrived at Harry's Bar in a sidecar.

Ingredients

3 ice cubes
1 measure cognac
1 measure Cointreau
1 measure freshly squeezed lemon juice
lemon zest spiral, to decorate

Method

Place the ice cubes into a cocktail shaker and pour over the cognac, Cointreau, and lemon juice. Shake for 30 seconds, then strain and pour into a chilled cocktail or old-fashioned glass (*see* pages 29–30). Decorate with the lemon spiral and serve.

ALTERNATIVE If liked, 1 teaspoon sugar syrup can be added.

New Yorker

SERVES 1

Ingredients

2 measures Scotch whisky
½ measure freshly squeezed lime juice
1 tsp. grenadine
4 ice cubes, crushed
orange slice, to decorate

Method

Place all the ingredients except the crushed ice into a cocktail shaker and shake for 1 minute. Place the crushed ice into an old-fashioned glass. Pour over the cocktail, decorate with an orange slice, and serve.

There seems to be little consensus on what traditionally constitutes a New Yorker, some recipes calling for claret instead of grenadine, but most flaunt a rich red color and they all provide a strong kick.

ALTERNATIVE Replace the Scotch whisky with bourbon and pour over ice cubes instead of crushed ice. Decorate with a lime twist.

Cosmopolitan

SERVES 1

Method 1

Ingredients

4 ice cubes, crushed
1 measure gin
½ measure Southern Comfort
½ measure black currant syrup
1 measure freshly squeezed lime juice
1 tsp. egg white
lime slice, to decorate

Method 2

Ingredients

4 ice cubes, crushed
1 measure vodka
1 measure Cointreau
1 measure cranberry juice
½ tsp. lemon juice
orange twist, to decorate

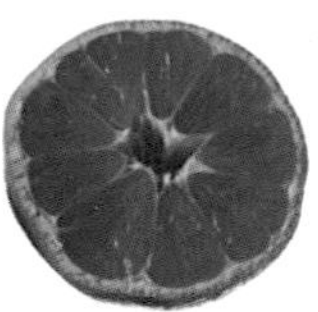

Several people have claimed to have devised, or been credited with creating, the "Cosmo." One of these is Cheryl Cook, a bartender from South Beach, Florida. In an online interview for the *Ardent Spirits* e-letter in October 2006, Cook states she created the drink in 1985 or 1986: "What overwhelmed me was the number of people who ordered Martinis just to be seen with a Martini glass in their hand. It was this realization that gave me the idea to create a drink that everyone could palate and was visually stunning in that classic glass. This is what the Cosmo was based on."

However, a certain Toby Cecchini is also involved. He developed a slightly different version, using Cointreau and freshly squeezed lime juice instead of Cook's Triple Sec and Rose's lime. This version has become the common standard method. There are, in fact, many variations on the Cosmopolitan, and here we have suggested a particularly different one, in addition to the more traditional.

Method 1

Place the crushed ice into a glass. Pour all the other ingredients into a cocktail shaker and shake for 1 minute, or until thoroughly blended. Strain into the ice-filled glass and serve decorated with a lime slice.

Method 2

Place all the ingredients except the ice into a cocktail shaker and shake for 20 seconds, or until blended. Place the crushed ice into an old-fashioned glass, pour the shaken cocktail over the crushed ice, then serve decorated with a twist of orange.

ALTERNATIVE Use lemon-flavored vodka with triple sec, cranberry juice, and freshly squeezed lime and lemon juices with a little honey.

Napoleon

SERVES 1

Ingredients

2–3 ice cubes, broken
2 measures gin
½ measure Dubonnet
2–3 dashes curaçao
dash Fernet Branca or Angostura bitters

Method

Place all the ingredients, except the ice into a cocktail shaker and shake for 1 minute, or until blended. Strain into an old-fashioned glass (*see* page 30) over the broken ice and serve immediately.

This cocktail contains Fernet Branca, which is an aromatic bitter liquor made from over 40 herbs and is mainly made these days in Milan.

ALTERNATIVE Try using Grand Marnier instead of curaçao, for a slightly sweeter taste.

Campari Delight

SERVES 2

Ingredients

1 large, ripe mango
6 measures mango juice
6 measures freshly squeezed orange juice
5 measures Campari
crushed ice
orange twists, to decorate
2 long cinnamon sticks, for stirring (optional)

Method

Peel the mango and cut the flesh away from the pit. Pass through a juicer into a pitcher. Mix the mango and orange juices together and stir in the Campari. Place some crushed ice in glasses, then pour over the prepared cocktail. Place an orange twist on the side of each glass, add a cinnamon stick to use as a stirrer, and serve immediately.

Cocktails are generally served before a meal, and it is quite normal to serve nibbles to help to alleviate the effects of the alcohol prior to eating. Potato chips and salsa would go well with this recipe.

ALTERNATIVE For a nonalcoholic version, increase the mango and orange juices to 1 cup each and omit the Campari. Add 2–3 tablespoons lime juice and a few dashes of Tabasco sauce.

Pink Gin

SERVES 1

Ingredients

4 dashes Angostura bitters
2 measures gin (Plymouth or London)
iced water

Method

Chill a glass until frosty. Pour in the Angostura bitters and swirl the glass until the bottom is coated with the bitters. Discard any remaining bitters. Pour in the gin, stir, and then serve with iced water and dilute to taste.

In 1824, a doctor who was treating the Venezuelan army for stomach ailments developed a remedy from locally grown bitter herbs. This later became known as Angostura bitters. It was the British Royal Navy who discovered a new use for the remedy by adding a few drops of gin; it gave the drink a whole new dimension.

ALTERNATIVE Replace the Angostura bitters with Angostura orange bitters and decorate with an orange twist.

White Lady

SERVES 1

Ingredients

2 measures gin
1 measure Cointreau
1 tsp. freshly squeezed lemon juice
½ tsp. egg white
2 ice cubes, crushed (optional)
lemon zest spiral, to decorate

Method

Place the gin, Cointreau, lemon juice, and egg white into a cocktail shaker and shake for 30 seconds until blended. Strain into a cocktail glass filled with the crushed ice, if using, and serve decorated with the lemon spiral.

This is a very popular classic cocktail that has a few varieties. Use either London or Plymouth gin, although these days London gin is more usual.

ALTERNATIVE Substitute the Cointreau with grenadine for a Pink Lady and the lemon juice with grapefruit juice for a Fair Lady.

Old–Fashioned

SERVES 1

Ingredients

2 measures bourbon
few drops Angostura bitters
few drops sugar syrup (*see* page 31)
orange slice and maraschino cherry, to decorate

Method

Place the bourbon, Angostura bitters, and sugar syrup in a cocktail shaker and shake for 30 seconds until blended. Pour into a chilled old-fashioned glass (*see* page 30) and serve decorated with the orange slice and cherry on a toothpick.

It is commonly believed that President Roosevelt mixed this cocktail for King George VI and Queen Elizabeth and it apparently went down a "storm."

ALTERNATIVE Fill the old-fashioned glass with crushed ice and pour the shaken cocktail over. Serve with a stirrer.

Collinson

SERVES 1

Ingredients

1 dash orange bitters
1 measure gin
½ measure dry vermouth
½–1 measure kirsch, according to taste
2 ice cubes, crushed
thinly pared lemon zest strip

Method

Place the orange bitters into a cocktail shaker with the gin and dry vermouth, and kirsch to taste. Shake for 30 seconds, then pour into a Collins glass (*see* page 30) filled with the crushed ice. Add the lemon zest and serve with a stirrer.

As its name suggests, this cocktail is based on the same format as a Collins, but it has an unusual twist with the addition of the kirsch. Orange bitters is a liqueur made from the peel of unripe or sour oranges steeped in gin or other alcohol.

ALTERNATIVE A delicious alternative is to replace the orange bitters with Angostura bitters and replace the kirsch with Cointreau. Use thinly pared orange zest instead of the lemon zest.

Salty Dog

SERVES 1

Ingredients

2 measures gin
4 measures grapefruit juice
4–5 ice cubes, broken
1 lime slice, to decorate

Method

Frost the glass (*see* page 31). Pour the gin and grapefruit juice into a cocktail shaker and shake for 30 seconds. Place the broken ice into a glass and strain in the gin and grapefruit. Decorate and serve immediately.

Give this cocktail a touch of sparkle by adding a margarita twist to the drink: frost the edge of the glass with grapefruit juice and salt. Let it dry before using.

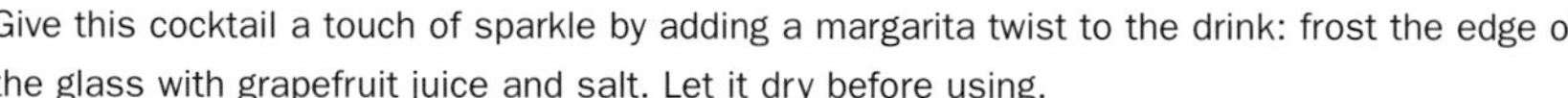

ALTERNATIVE To make a Greyhound, serve in a plain glass and replace the gin with vodka.

Between the Sheets

SERVES 1

Often, a cocktail is served chilled but without the ice being present in the serving glass. This is achieved by placing the ingredients and crushed ice into a cocktail shaker and then shaking until a frost forms on the outside. The cocktail is then strained into the glass.

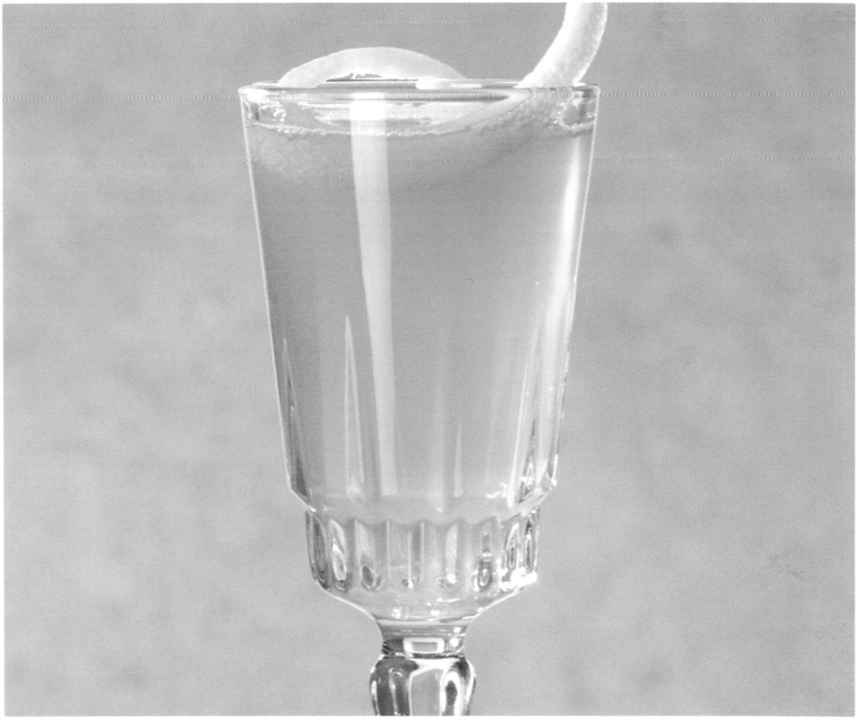

Ingredients

4 ice cubes, crushed
1½ measures brandy
1 measure white rum
½ measure Cointreau
1 tsp. freshly squeezed lemon juice
1 tsp. sugar syrup (*see* page 31)
lemon butterfly twist, to decorate

Method

Place the crushed ice with the brandy, white rum, Cointreau, lemon juice, and sugar syrup in a cocktail shaker. Shake for 1 minute, or until thoroughly chilled and a frost appears on the outside of the shaker. Strain into a cocktail glass, decorate, and serve.

ALTERNATIVE Omit the sugar syrup for a cocktail with more bite.

Beachcomber

SERVES 1

Ingredients

3 ice cubes, crushed
1 measure green crème de menthe
4 measures club soda or lemon-flavor soda
1 mint sprig, to decorate

Method

Place the crushed ice into a glass and pour over the crème de menthe. Top off with the club soda or soda and stir. Decorate with a mint sprig and serve immediately.

A cool, refreshing drink that is ideal on a long, hot, sunny day. Try serving at summer parties without much alcohol content, because it is perfect for keeping the heat out without ruining the party mood.

ALTERNATIVE For a more alcoholic version, add 1 measure of rum and 1 of triple sec with 1 tablespoon of maraschino liqueur.

Sea Breeze

SERVES 1

Ingredients

1 measure vodka
2–3 measures, or to taste, cranberry juice
1–2 measures, or to taste, grapefruit juice
4 ice cubes
orange slice and fresh cranberries, if available, to decorate

Method

Place the vodka in a cocktail shaker and add the cranberry and grapefruit juices to taste. Shake until blended. Place the ice into a glass, pour the cocktail over, and serve decorated with an orange slice and a stirrer.

Back in the 1930s, this cocktail was made with gin, grenadine, and lemon juice. However, over the years, it has developed into this popular and, it has to be said, delicious cocktail.

ALTERNATIVE Replace the grapefruit juice with pineapple juice to make a Bay Breeze.

Harvey Wallbanger

SERVES 1

Ingredients

6–8 ice cubes
½ measure Galliano
1½ measures vodka
5 measures freshly squeezed orange juice
2 small orange wedges, to decorate

There are a few stories regarding the naming of this famous drink. One of them relates to Harvey, a Californian surfer who added Galliano to a Screwdriver—he loved it so much he ordered quite a few. On trying to leave, he bounced and bumped his way out from one wall to the next until he found the door—hence the Harvey Wallbanger was born.

Method

Place some ice cubes into a Collins glass (*see* page 30) and pour over the Galliano. Place the vodka, orange juice, and remaining ice into a cocktail shaker and shake until frosty. Strain, then pour over the Galliano, decorate, and serve with a stirrer.

ALTERNATIVE If liked, pour the chilled vodka and orange over crushed ice, then carefully pour the Galliano on top so it floats on the surface.

Rum Planter Cocktail

SERVES 1

Ingredients

4 ice cubes, crushed
1 measure dark rum
1 tsp. freshly squeezed orange juice
1 tsp. freshly squeezed lemon juice
2 dashes Angostura bitters
1 tsp. superfine sugar
tropical fruits, to decorate, such as pineapple, mango, and banana

Method

Place the crushed ice into a cocktail shaker and add the rum with the orange and lemon juices, together with the Angostura bitters and sugar. Shake for 1 minute, or until a frost is formed on the outside of the shaker. Pour into a glass and decorate with small pieces of pineapple, mango, and banana.

When a recipe calls for a little freshly squeezed citrus fruit, simply cut a small or medium wedge of fruit and place in a hand-held squeezer, or just squeeze using your fingers.

ALTERNATIVE Vary the fruits used to decorate. For a special occasion, make a stunning decoration by threading small pieces of mango, kiwi, pineapple, and papaya onto a short kebab stick and balance across the glass.

Sex on the Beach

SERVES 1

Ingredients

½ measure vodka
½ measure peach schnapps
1 measure cranberry juice
1 measure freshly squeezed orange juice
3 ice cubes
1 peach slice, to decorate (optional)

Method

Place all the ingredients into a cocktail shaker and shake for 30–45 seconds. Pour into a chilled tall glass, serve decorated with the peach slice, and add a straw.

If you are holding a party and there are a few of the same cocktail required, double up the ingredients to reduce the waiting time, especially at the beginning of the party.

ALTERNATIVE For more variety, swap the peach decoration for a maraschino cherry and orange slice.

Adonis

SERVES 1

Ingredients

2 measures dry sherry (Tio Pepe)
1 measure sweet rosso vermouth
1–2 dashes orange bitters or orange curaçao
thinly pared orange zest spiral, to decorate

Method

Place all the ingredients except the orange zest into a cocktail shaker and blend for 20 seconds. Pour into a cocktail glass and serve decorated with the orange zest spiral.

Created in 1886 to celebrate the success of a Broadway show, this cocktail quickly became popular both in the United States and the UK. If you like a sweet drink, use sweet sherry, otherwise use the dry sherry, such as Tio Pepe, as used in this recipe.

ALTERNATIVE Use 1 dash Angostura bitters, if liked, in place of the orange bitters.

Tequila Sunrise

SERVES 1

Ingredients

4 ice cubes
½ measure grenadine
2 measures tequila
5 measures freshly squeezed orange juice
orange slice and maraschino cherry, to decorate

Method

Place the crushed ice into a tall glass and then slowly pour the grenadine over the ice, letting it sink to the bottom of the glass. Place the tequila and orange juice in a cocktail shaker and shake for 30 seconds. Strain into the glass and serve decorated with an orange slice, a maraschino cherry, and a straw.

As the name suggests, this cocktail originated in Mexico around 1930. It was called Tequila Sunrise most probably due to the colors that are caught in the glass, which are similar to the beautiful sunrises found in Mexico.

ALTERNATIVE Try a Florida Sunrise: simply replace the orange juice with pineapple juice and decorate with a small pineapple wedge.

Zombie

SERVES 1

Ingredients

3 ice cubes
1 measure dark rum
1 measure white rum
½ measure apricot brandy
2 measures pineapple juice
2 measures freshly squeezed orange juice
1 measure lime juice
pineapple wedge, maraschino cherry and mint sprig, to decorate

Method

Place the ice into a cocktail shaker, then pour in the other ingredients. Shake for 30 seconds, then pour into a glass and serve decorated with a pineapple wedge, cherry, and mint sprig. Serve immediately and add a straw to the glass.

Created in 1933 in America's very first South Sea Island restaurant in order to complement the exotic food that was to be served there, this quickly became a great hit and other similar beach restaurants soon sprang up.

ALTERNATIVE If liked, frost the rim of the glass with lime juice and salt (*see* page 31).

007 Vodka Martini

SERVES 1

Ingredients

3 measures vodka
1 measure dry vermouth (such as Noilly Prat)
lemon twist
1 green olive, to decorate

Method

Place the vodka into a cocktail shaker and pour in the dry vermouth. Shake for 20 seconds and pour into a cocktail glass. Squeeze over the lemon twist to release a few drops of juice, then discard. Finally, decorate with the green olive on a toothpick.

This cocktail was made famous by the movie star Sean Connery while playing James Bond when, in the movie, he says these immortal words: "Mine's a vodka Martini, shaken, not stirred." Purists, however, would argue that a Martini should in fact be stirred, not shaken. Whichever you choose—enjoy.

ALTERNATIVE Gin can be used in place of the vodka, as can Bacardi rum.

Gin & It

SERVES 1

Ingredients

4 measures sweet rosso vermouth
1 measure gin
1 ice cube (optional)
1 maraschino cherry, to decorate

This cocktail could be described as the original Martini, and the first mention of a Martini was in 1862 with a drink called Martinez. This drink was made from sweet vermouth and gin. Gradually, the sweet vermouth was replaced with dry vermouth and the Dry Martini was born. Gin & It was very popular in the 1940s and drunk mainly by women both during and after the Second World War.

Method

Place the sweet vermouth and gin into a cocktail shaker and shake for 30 seconds. Pour into a short glass, add the ice, if using, and decorate with the maraschino cherry.

ALTERNATIVE If liked, try shaking with broken ice before straining into the glass.

Celery & Cucumber Martini

SERVES 2–4

Whether you shake or stir this Martini, once you have offered one to your friends, be prepared to make plenty more.

Ingredients

2 young celery stalks
½ English cucumber
few mint sprigs
6 measures white Bacardi rum
2 measures white vermouth
crushed ice, to serve
2–4 green olives, to decorate

Method

Trim the celery of all the leaves. Cut into small chunks. Peel the cucumber, cut in half, and discard the seeds. Chop. Place all the ingredients except the crushed ice and olives in a smoothie machine or blender. If using a smoothie machine, blend on mix for 15 seconds and then on smooth for 45 seconds. If using a blender, blend for 1–2 minutes until smooth. Place crushed ice in glasses, pour over the cocktail, and serve immediately with the olives on toothpicks.

ALTERNATIVE Replace the white Bacardi rum and white vermouth with ginger beer for a nonalcoholic version.

Merry Widow

SERVES 1

Ingredients

2 measures gin
1 measure dry vermouth
1 tsp. Bénédictine
½ tsp. Pernod
1 dash Angostura bitters

Method

Place all the ingredients into a cocktail shaker and shake for 30 seconds. Strain into a cocktail glass and serve.

This cocktail is a mixture of cultures. One of the components of vermouth is the herb wormwood, which, if taken in large quantities, can cause hallucinations. The sweet vermouth was developed in Italy in the eighteenth century, while, later, in the nineteenth century, the French developed the dry vermouth.

ALTERNATIVE For a delicious change, try a measure of cherry brandy, a measure of maraschino liqueur, a dash of orange bitters, shaken, and poured over crushed ice. Decorate with a maraschino cherry.

Bacardi Classic

SERVES 1

It was in 1936 that a New York hotel bar and restaurant started serving this cocktail without using Bacardi rum. After a visit by the makers of Bacardi rum to the courts, a temporary injunction was raised and later that year became permanent at the Supreme Court, which stated that *only* Bacardi rum should be used for this cocktail.

Ingredients

1½–2 measures Bacardi rum
1 measure lemon juice
1 tsp. grenadine
1 tsp., or to taste, sugar syrup (*see* page 31)
2 ice cubes, crushed
1 maraschino cherry

Method

Place all the ingredients into a cocktail shaker and shake for 30 seconds. Pour into a cocktail glass and serve decorated with the cherry on a toothpick.

ALTERNATIVE Use the full 2 measures Bacardi rum if a stronger drink is preferred, and replace the lemon juice with lime juice.

Gimlet

SERVES 1

Ingredients

2 measures gin
1 tbsp. freshly squeezed lime juice or syrup
2 ice cubes, crushed
1 measure club soda
lime twist, to decorate

Method

Place the gin and lime juice into a cocktail shaker and shake for 20 seconds. Place the crushed glass ice into an old-fashioned and strain over the cocktail. Add the club soda and serve with a lime twist and a stirrer.

A gimlet is a small tool that is used to bore holes in wood and was often used by innkeepers to tap into barrels. Cocktails bearing the name Gimlet appeared around 1930 and it was used to describe a short sharp drink.

ALTERNATIVE Vodka, tequila, and rum can all be used to replace the gin to suit any taste.

Brandy Classic

SERVES 1

Ingredients

1 measure brandy
1 measure blue curaçao
1 tbsp. freshly squeezed lemon juice
1 tbsp. syrup from a jar of maraschino cherries
3 ice cubes, crushed
lemon zest spiral and maraschino cherry, to decorate

Method

Place all the ingredients into a cocktail shaker and shake for 30 seconds. Pour into a cocktail glass and serve decorated with the lemon zest spiral and a maraschino cherry.

This cocktail gets its color by the addition of blue curaçao. This attractive liqueur comes from the dried peel of the green orange that is grown on the Caribbean island of the same name.

ALTERNATIVE Try replacing the brandy with either gin or vodka or even white rum.

Luigi

SERVES 1

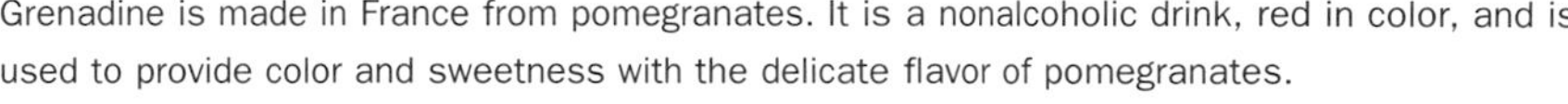

Grenadine is made in France from pomegranates. It is a nonalcoholic drink, red in color, and is used to provide color and sweetness with the delicate flavor of pomegranates.

Ingredients

1 measure freshly squeezed orange juice
1 measure dry vermouth
½ measure Cointreau
1 measure grenadine
2 measures gin
3 ice cubes
orange wedge, to decorate

Method

Place all the ingredients into a cocktail shaker and shake for 30 seconds, or until a frost forms on the outside of the shaker. Strain into a cocktail glass and serve decorated with an orange wedge and a stirrer.

ALTERNATIVE Replace the grenadine with the juice from a freshly squeezed pomegranate, strained into the cocktail shaker to remove any seeds. Pour over crushed ice and decorate the glass with a thin wedge of pomegranate.

French Leave

SERVES 1

Ingredients

2 ice cubes, crushed
2 measures vodka
1 measure Pernod
1 measure freshly squeezed orange juice
maraschino cherry, mint sprig, and peach slice, to decorate

Method

Place the ingredients in a cocktail shaker and shake for 30 seconds, or until a frost forms on the outside of the shaker. Strain into a cocktail glass and serve, decorated with a maraschino cherry, mint sprig, and peach slice.

Pernod is made from the spice star anise that can be found in North Vietnam and Southern China. It is an aromatic spice used extensively in these areas to flavor many traditional dishes as well as drinks.

ALTERNATIVE Replace the vodka with either brandy or gin.

Opera

SERVES 1

Ingredients

4 ice cubes
1 measure Dubonnet
½ measure yellow curaçao
2 measures gin
orange and lemon zest spirals, to decorate

Method

Place 2 ice cubes into the cocktail shaker with the Dubonnet, curaçao, and gin. Shake for 30 seconds. Place the remaining ice cubes into a cocktail glass, pour over the Dubonnet and gin, and serve decorated with the orange and lemon zest spirals and a stirrer.

In the 1960s, Dubonnet became a popular drink, especially with women, but it now seems to have lost popularity as a drink on its own. However, it makes an excellent addition to any cocktail. A red wine-based drink that is flavored with an extract from the bark of a tropical tree, it was developed in France by Joseph Dubonnet around 1846.

ALTERNATIVE Have fun by using one of the other varieties of curaçao—try blue, green, or even red.

Stormy Weather

SERVES 1

Ingredients

2–3 ice cubes
2 measures gin
½ measure Mandarine Napoléon liqueur
½ measure dry vermouth
1 measure sweet rosso vermouth
orange twist, to decorate

Method

Place the ice cubes in a cocktail shaker with all the other ingredients. Shake for 30 seconds, or until a frost forms on the outside of the cocktail shaker. Strain into a cocktail glass and serve decorated with an orange twist and a stirrer.

Sweet vermouth is an aromatic, reddish brown wine-based drink originating from Italy and was developed in the eighteenth century. These days, Martini Rosso and Cinzano are the most easily obtained sweet vermouths.

ALTERNATIVE There are a few different versions of this cocktail. Here is one other. Use 2 measures dark rum, 5 measures ginger beer, and 1 measure lime juice. Shake, pour over crushed ice, and serve with a stirrer and lime twist.

Black Widow

SERVES 1

Ingredients

3 ice cubes
2 measures dark rum
1–1½ measures Southern Comfort
freshly squeezed lime juice
1 tsp. sugar syrup (*see* page 31)
lime slice

Method

Place the ice cubes in a cocktail shaker with all the other ingredients. Shake for 30 seconds, then strain into a cocktail glass and serve decorated with the lime slice.

This cocktail has a definite kick to it and is not for the faint-hearted, combining the fruity flavors of peach and orange with a distinct hint of herbs and a good splash of Southern Comfort. Guaranteed to get any party going.

ALTERNATIVE Try a slice of lemon, instead of lime, to decorate.

Mad Dog

SERVES 1

Ingredients

3–4 ice cubes
1 measure tequila
1 measure crème de banane
1 measure dark crème de cacao
freshly squeezed juice from ½ lime
lime wedge and banana slice, to decorate

Method

Place the ice cubes in a cocktail shaker and add the other ingredients. Shake for 30 seconds, or until a frost forms on the outside of the shaker. Strain into a cocktail glass and serve decorated with the lime wedge and banana slice.

Crème de cacao is a chocolate liqueur and is normally made as a clear, light liquid, but can be found as a dark, caramel color. The delicious chocolate flavor is obtained from both the cocoa bean and the vanilla bean. The alcoholic content can vary and is often as high as 25 percent.

ALTERNATIVE Try white crème de cacao for a different effect.

Negroni

SERVES 1

Ingredients

1 measure gin
1 measure sweet rosso vermouth
½ measure Campari
3 ice cubes, broken
1 measure club soda
orange twist, to decorate

Method

Place the gin, sweet vermouth, and Campari into a cocktail shaker and shake until blended. Fill a short glass three-quarters full with broken ice and pour over the gin-and-vermouth mixture. Add the club soda, decorate, and serve.

Campari comes from an infusion of bitter herbs, aromatic plants, and fruits that are steeped in alcohol and water; it is classed with the "bitters." This cocktail originated in Italy around 1860 and its 60 ingredients are still a closely guarded secret, even to this day.

ALTERNATIVE For a long, cooling drink, replace the Campari with orange bitters, pour over crushed ice into a tall glass and top off with club soda.

Crossbow

SERVES 1

Ingredients

1 tbsp. finely grated chocolate
3 ice cubes
½ measure gin
½ measure dark crème de cacao
½ measure Cointreau

Method

Place the grated chocolate on a saucer and pour 2 tablespoons water into another. Dip a chilled cocktail glass in the water and then in the grated chocolate in order to coat the rim. Let set for 5 minutes before using. Place the ice cubes in the cocktail shaker and pour in the gin, crème de cacao, and Cointreau. Shake until well blended, then pour into the chocolate-rimmed glass and serve.

Decorating the rim of the glass is a fun thing to do and adds to the general mood of the party, showing your guests that you care. Try to vary the ingredients used, such as unsweetened cocoa, sugar, salt, or even a ground spice such as cinnamon or allspice.

ALTERNATIVE Make a white instead of dark Crossbow cocktail. Use finely grated white chocolate to decorate the rim of the glass and replace the dark crème de cacao with white crème de cacao.

Skipper

SERVES 1

Ingredients

3 ice cubes
½ measure grenadine
1 measure dry vermouth
3–4 measures Scotch whisky
freshly squeezed juice from ½ orange, preferably organic
orange twist, to decorate

Method

Place the ice cubes in a cocktail shaker and add the grenadine, dry vermouth, whisky, and orange juice. Shake for about 30 seconds, then pour into a short glass and serve decorated with the orange twist.

There are many brands of Scotch whiskey blends to choose from, so, when using whiskey for cocktails, use whichever you prefer, but it's better to drink the malts without accompaniment.

ALTERNATIVE Look out for Skipper's Ripper—a different drink containing cola, grenadine, rum, and Southern Comfort.

Sours & Juleps

Brandy Sour

SERVES 1

It is widely believed that the first Brandy Sour to be mixed was around 1850 and was the beginning of a whole new drink experience. As the name implies, they contain very little sweetness and a large amount of lemon juice or similar sour flavoring.

Ingredients

3–4 ice cubes
2–3 dashes Angostura bitters
3 tbsp. freshly squeezed lemon juice
3 measures brandy
1 tsp. sugar syrup (*see* page 31)
lemon twist, to decorate

Method

Put the ice cubes into a cocktail shaker and sprinkle in the Angostura bitters. Add the lemon juice, brandy, and sugar syrup and shake for 1 minute, or until a frost is formed on the outside of the shaker. Strain into a glass and serve decorated with a lemon twist.

ALTERNATIVE Replace the brandy with whiskey.

Vodka Sour

SERVES 1

Ingredients

6 ice cubes
2 measures vodka
½ measure sugar syrup (*see* page 31)
1 egg white, preferably organic
2 measures freshly squeezed lemon juice
3 drops Angostura bitters (optional)
club soda
lemon zest spiral, to decorate

Method

Place 2 ice cubes in a cocktail shaker and add the vodka, sugar syrup, and egg white. Shake briefly before adding the lemon juice and bitters, if using, and shaking for 30 seconds, or until a frost is formed on the outside of the shaker. Place the remaining ice cubes in a highball glass, strain over the vodka mixture, top off the glass with club soda, and serve decorated with the lemon zest spiral and a stirrer.

For a change, serve a sour as a long drink. Make as usual and then pour over 4–6 ice cubes placed in a highball glass (*see* page 30). Top off with club soda and serve with a stirrer.

ALTERNATIVE This method would work with all sours, if liked.

Amaretto Sour

SERVES 1

Ingredients

2 ice cubes
1½ measures amaretto liqueur
1½ measures freshly squeezed lemon juice
1 tsp. sugar syrup (*see* *page 31*)
lemon twist, to decorate

Method

Place the ice in a cocktail shaker and add the amaretto, lemon juice, and sugar syrup. Shake for 30 seconds, or until a frost forms on the outside. Strain into a small glass and serve decorated with a lemon twist.

Amaretto is a sweet liqueur made from a basic infusion of almonds or of the kernels from the drupe fruit. It has a very distinctive almond or marzipan aroma and flavor. There are a few brands available, but the best-known is Amaretto Disaronno.

ALTERNATIVE Prepared sweet-and-sour mixes are an easy alternative to lime juice and sugar syrup.

Egg Sour

SERVES 1

Ingredients

1 measure brandy
1 measure dry orange curaçao
1½ measures freshly squeezed lemon juice
1 very fresh medium egg, lightly whisked
2 ice cubes, crushed
lemon slice, to decorate

Method

Place the brandy in a cocktail shaker with the orange curaçao, lemon juice, lightly whisked egg, and crushed ice. Shake for 20 seconds, then strain into a short glass and serve decorated with a lemon slice.

With this recipe, it is important that the egg is particularly fresh. Do make sure that you prepare this cocktail when it is required, and do not leave it standing around. Shake and serve—that is the trick with this cocktail.

ALTERNATIVE Add fine sugar to the shaker to sweeten, to taste.

Bourbon Triple Sour

SERVES 1

Triple sec is an almost colorless orange-flavor liqueur developed by Jean-Baptiste Combier around 1834 in Saumur, one of the towns situated on the banks of the Loire River in France. It is used in many drinks, mainly as a sweetener, and also adds a hint of orange flavor.

Ingredients

1 measure bourbon
1 measure triple sec
1½ measures freshly squeezed lemon juice
1 tsp. sugar syrup (*see* page 31)
3 ice cubes, broken
lime slice and maraschino cherry, to decorate

Method

Pour the bourbon, triple sec, lemon juice, and sugar syrup into a cocktail shaker and shake for 20 seconds. Fill a glass with the broken ice, then strain the cocktail into the glass and serve decorated with the lime slice and maraschino cherry and add a stirrer.

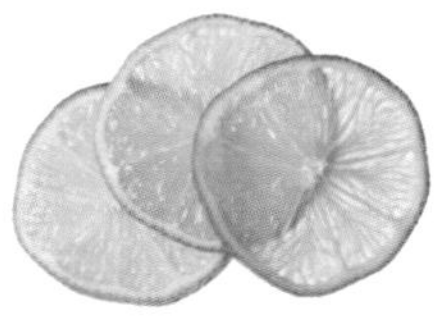

ALTERNATIVE Replace the bourbon with Scotch whisky and use orange instead of lemon juice. Pour over crushed ice and decorate with a twist of orange zest.

Southern Tango

SERVES 1

Ingredients

4 ice cubes
1 measure dry vermouth
1 measure Southern Comfort
2 measures lemon-flavor soda

Method

When ready to serve, fill the cocktail shaker with the ice cubes and pour in the dry vermouth with the Southern Comfort. Shake for 30 seconds, then strain into the ice-filled glass. Top off with the soda and serve immediately with a stirrer.

Many of the cocktails demand crushed ice. It is important that the water used to make the ice is of good drinking quality, otherwise, as the ice melts into the cocktail, it could affect the taste of the drink.

ALTERNATIVE To make this a true sour, pour the dry vermouth with the Southern Comfort and 2 measures freshly strained lemon juice and 1 teaspoon, or to taste, sugar syrup into a cocktail shaker. Shake all the ingredients together and serve in a short glass.

Caipirinha

SERVES 1

Ingredients

1 lime
1½–2 tsp. superfine sugar
4 ice cubes, broken
2 measures cachaça

Caipirinha is the national cocktail of Brazil and is normally made with the country's favorite brandy, cachaça, which is made from sugar cane. Caipirinhas and other tropical cocktails are usually made with unaged cachaça, but aged cachaça is also available. Aged cachaça comes in shades ranging from gold to amber and deserves to be sipped, like a fine tequila or single malt Scotch.

The word *caipirinha* is the diminutive form of *caipira*, meaning "peasant" or "country person," but, in its feminine form, it signifies the cocktail first and foremost (Brazilians rarely associate it with country people). Caipirinhas are now popular across the world and have been labeled one of the 50 greatest drinks of all time by the International Bartender Association. It is made directly in the glass, never in a cocktail shaker.

Method

Cut the lime into small wedges and place with the sugar into an old-fashioned glass (*see* page 30). Using a spoon, crush the lime wedges and sugar together until the juice flows out of the lime. Add sufficient broken ice to fill the glass, then top off with the cachaça and serve.

ALTERNATIVE Many varieties of this cocktail are served the length and breadth of Brazil. These are often served with a variety of fruits in place of the lime. Try passion fruits, kiwi, pineapple, raspberries and other berries, or grapes. Sometimes milk is added, giving a creamy cocktail. Another alternative can be made using vodka.

Scotch Melon Sour

SERVES 1

Midori, with its bright green color, is a melon-flavored liqueur, and is an excellent addition to any drink. Being extremely sweet, it is often added to such drinks as sours to help modify the bitter tang. Vary the amount used to suit individual taste.

Ingredients

4 ice cubes
1 measure Scotch whisky
1 measure Midori
2 measures freshly squeezed lemon juice
1 tsp. sugar syrup (*see* page 31)

Method

Put the ice cubes into an old-fashioned glass (*see* page 30) or other glass, if preferred. Pour the remaining ingredients into a cocktail shaker and shake for 30 seconds, then strain into the ice-filled glass and serve with a stirrer.

ALTERNATIVE Use other fruit-based liqueurs in place of the Midori; try kirsch, Cointreau, or framboise.

Pisco Sour

SERVES 1

Ingredients

3 ice cubes, crushed
½–1 measure freshly squeezed lime juice
2 measures pisco
1 tsp. sugar syrup (*see* page 31)
2 tsp. egg white, preferably organic, lightly whisked
1 dash Angostura bitters
lime wedge, to decorate

Method

Place the crushed ice in a glass, then squeeze the lime juice over the crushed ice. Pour the remaining ingredients into a cocktail shaker and shake for 30 seconds. Pour over the ice and serve decorated with a lime wedge.

Pisco is a brandy that is made by distilling Muscat wine. It has been an integral part of Peruvian culture for many years and, even if no wine is consumed during a meal, it is inconceivable not to have a glass of pisco after the meal.

ALTERNATIVE Try using ½ measure of both lemon and lime juice and add 2 measures whiskey, 1 measure triple sec, and ½ measure pineapple juice to the other ingredients.

Rob Roy

SERVES 1

This cocktail is named after the Scottish hero Rob Roy, who lived in the seventeenth century and has been described by many as the Scottish Robin Hood.

Ingredients

1–2 ice cubes, broken
1 measure Scotch whisky
1 measure sweet vermouth
2 dashes Angostura bitters
lemon zest spiral and maraschino cherry, to decorate

Method

Place the broken ice in an old-fashioned glass, then pour the remaining ingredients into a cocktail shaker and shake for 30 seconds. Pour over the ice and serve decorated with the lemon zest spiral and maraschino cherry.

ALTERNATIVE For a Dry Rob Roy, use dry instead of sweet vermouth; or, for a Perfect Rob Roy, use equal parts sweet and dry vermouth.

Scorpio

SERVES 1

Ingredients

5 ice cubes, crushed
1 measure brandy
½ measure white rum
½ measure dark rum
2 measures freshly squeezed orange juice
½ measure Amaretto Disaronno
2–3 dashes Angostura bitters

Method

Place half the ice in a cocktail shaker and add the brandy, white and dark rums, orange juice, Amaretto Disaronno, and Angostura bitters. Shake for 1 minute, or until a frost is formed on the outside of the shaker. Strain into a glass, add the remaining crushed ice, and serve with a stirrer.

When serving cocktails, presentation is very important; be careful when cutting fruit twists to discard any seeds and keep the slice thin but still intact. It is a good idea to cut some decorations in advance, then cover lightly and keep in the refrigerator.

ALTERNATIVE Use all dark or white rum, if preferred.

Mojito

SERVES 1

Ingredients

4 ice cubes, crushed
2–3 mint sprigs, plus 1 fresh mint sprig to decorate
2 measures white rum
3 tbsp. freshly squeezed lime juice
2 tsp., or to taste, raw sugar
club soda

One of the most popular summer cocktails around today. This drink has become the "wow" both in New York and London, regardless of the weather. The name supposedly comes from the African word *mojo*, a type of magic charm, but the drink is undisputedly Cuban. Legend has it that it was invented at La Bodeguita del Medio in Havana and that Ernest Hemingway would refresh himself there with mojitos after a long day's fishing—apparently coining the phrase, "I drink my mojito in La Bodeguita and my daiquiri in El Floridita."

Others claim that the mojito's origins stretch far back to the swashbuckling days of Sir Francis Drake, and that the pirate Richard Drake invented a mojito-like drink using aquardiente (an unrefined forerunner of rum), calling it "El Draque." There are many variations, and part of the fun is experimenting with the ingredients to discover which ones best suit your taste.

Method

Place half the crushed ice in a glass and add the mint sprigs. Carefully crush the mint on the ice. Pour the rum, lime juice, sugar, and remaining ice into a cocktail shaker and shake until a frost forms on the outside. Pour into the glass, top off with club soda, decorate with a fresh mint sprig, and serve with a stirrer.

ALTERNATIVE Try using other flavored rums, such as dark rum, or even fruit-flavor rums, such as mango-flavor rum.

Clover Club

SERVES 1

This pre-Prohibition-era drink apparently dates back to at least 1911 and is named after a Philadelphia men's club of the same name. This drink is very similar to a Pink Lady, which uses cream or applejack instead of the lemon juice, depending on which recipe you choose.

Ingredients

3 ice cubes
1½ measures gin
1 measure freshly squeezed lemon juice
1–2 tsp., or to taste, grenadine
1 small egg white, preferably organic, lightly whisked

Method

Place the ice in a cocktail shaker and add the remaining ingredients. Shake for 30 seconds, then strain into a cocktail glass and serve.

ALTERNATIVE Add 3 mint sprigs to a glass filled halfway with crushed ice and lightly crush the mint on the ice. Mix the cocktail as above, then pour over the mint-flavored crushed ice. This then becomes a Clover Leaf.

Vodka Sazerac

SERVES 1

Ingredients

1 sugar cube
2 drops Angostura bitters
3 drops Pernod
2 measures vodka
3 ice cubes, broken
lemon-flavor soda
lemon slice, to decorate (optional)

Method

Place the sugar cube in an old-fashioned glass (*see* page 30) and add the Angostura bitters and Pernod. Using a stirrer, push the sugar cube around the glass. Add the vodka and the ice cubes, stir, then top off with the soda. Add the lemon slice to the glass, if using, and serve.

Originally made with brandy, and, later, rye whiskey, the Sazerac is reputed to be the first ever cocktail. It was developed by a Creole immigrant, Antoine Peychaud, who also created Peychaud bitters. The cocktail was later adopted by the Cubans.

ALTERNATIVE Try experimenting and use different-flavor vodkas; choose a fruit flavor, such as orange, lemon, peach, or even a herb, but keep in mind the aniseed flavor of the Pernod.

Mint Julep

SERVES 1

The word "julep" is thought to have come from an ancient Arabic word meaning "rose water." It was not until the eighteenth century that the first mention of julep occurred in the United States and it quickly caught on, so that, by the nineteenth century, it had been thoroughly Americanized.

Ingredients

4 fresh mint sprigs
1 measure sugar syrup (*see* page 31)
3 measures bourbon
4 ice cubes, crushed
2–3 fresh mint sprigs, to decorate

Method

Place the mint sprigs in a glass and add the sugar syrup. With the back of a bar spoon, gently crush the mint into the sugar syrup to extract the mint flavor. Remove the crushed sprigs. Slowly stir in the bourbon, then add the crushed ice. Place the fresh mint with the stalks down and the leaves facing upward in the glass. Serve with a straw.

ALTERNATIVE Some mint juleps are served without crushing the mint into the sugar syrup. Simply fill a glass with crushed ice and pour over the sugar syrup, then slowly stir in the bourbon. Add the mint sprigs and serve.

Southern Mint Julep

SERVES 1

Ingredients

5 fresh mint sprigs
1 measure sugar syrup (*see* *page 31*)
1 measure Kentucky bourbon
3 measures Southern Comfort
4 ice cubes, crushed

Method

Reserve 1 mint sprig to decorate, then place the rest in a glass and add the sugar syrup. Slowly stir in the bourbon and Southern Comfort, then add the crushed ice. Decorate and serve with a straw and a stirrer.

The Southern Mint Julep is as its name implies, synonymous with the states in the South. Traditionally, juleps were served in silver or pewter cups and held by the drinker only at the bottom and top edge of the cup. This let a frost form on the outside of the cup, and was meant to portray gentility.

ALTERNATIVE A traditional mint julep is made with four ingredients: mint, bourbon, sugar, and water. Spearmint is the variety of mint most commonly used.

Champagne Julep

SERVES 1

In the United States, juleps were originally made with brandy instead of bourbon and, with this recipe, brandy is the ideal spirit to use with champagne.

Ingredients

- 1–2 ice cubes, crushed
- 1 measure sugar syrup (*see* page 31)
- 2 measures brandy
- 3 measures champagne
- 2–3 fresh mint sprigs, to decorate

Method

Place the crushed ice in a champagne flute and pour over the sugar syrup and then the brandy. Gently pour in the champagne and add the mint sprigs, with the leaves facing uppermost. Stir gently with a stirrer and serve.

ALTERNATIVE Although brandy is best, bourbon can be used instead.

Jungle Juice

SERVES 1

Ingredients

4 ice cubes, crushed
2 whole ice cubes
1 measure Pisang Ambon
½ measure brandy
1 measure gin
4 measures freshly squeezed orange juice
2 tsp. freshly squeezed lemon juice
3 mint sprigs

Method

Place all the ingredients except for the crushed ice into a cocktail shaker. Shake for 1 minute, or until a frost forms on the outside of the cocktail shaker. Strain into an old-fashioned glass, then add the crushed ice and the mint sprigs with the leaves pointing up and serve.

Pisang Ambon is a very sweet, bright green liqueur from Indonesia and is made from herbs and green bananas. It works well when blended with orange juice or orange-flavored liqueur, such as Cointreau.

ALTERNATIVE Add 1 measure Cointreau to the above cocktail and top off the glass with club soda.

Jungle Wild

SERVES 1

Ingredients

4 ice cubes, crushed
1 measure white rum
1 measure Wild Turkey bourbon
½ measure Pisang Ambon
2 measures papaya juice
2 tbsp. freshly squeezed lime juice
2 measures lemon-flavored soda
3 fresh mint sprigs

Method

Place the crushed ice in a glass and pour over the white rum and Wild Turkey bourbon with the Pisang Ambon. Stir with a bar spoon, then add the papaya juice and the strained lime juice. Top off with the soda and decorate with mint sprigs.

When using fresh mint or any herb to decorate a drink, it is important to ensure that the herb is clean and free from any insects. Check carefully and, if necessary, rinse lightly, gently brushing off any dirt with your fingers, then allow it to dry on paper towels before using.

ALTERNATIVE Thread some papaya wedges onto a shortened kebab stick and place across the top of the glass.

Knockout

SERVES 1

Ingredients

4 ice cubes, crushed
2–3 mint sprigs
1 measure dry vermouth
1 measure white crème de menthe
2 measures gin
1 dash Pernod
lime slice, to decorate

Method

Place the crushed ice in a glass and add the mint sprigs, dry vermouth, and crème de menthe. Stir gently with a bar spoon, then slowly stir in the gin and Pernod. Stir again, then decorate with the lime slice and serve.

The joy of this white cocktail is the surprise of the cool, delicious mint flavor. If you cannot find white crème de menthe, use the green variety; the flavor will be the same, just the color will be different (and the mint flavor less of a surprise!).

ALTERNATIVE For a more colorful drink, replace the white crème de menthe with green crème de menthe, use Anis liqueur in place of the Pernod, and add a cherry instead of a lime slice.

Champagne & Sparkles

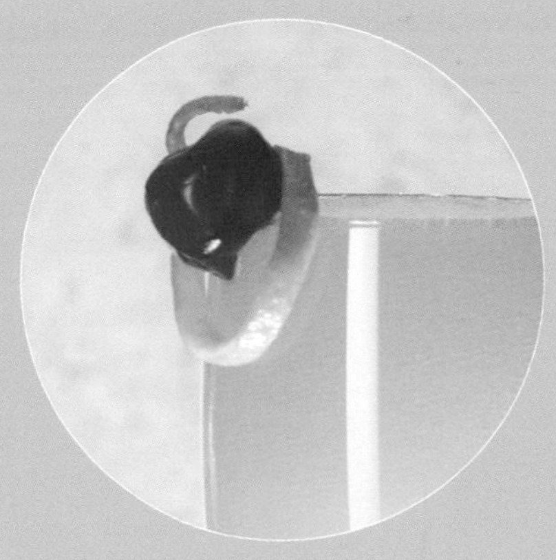

Kir Royale

SERVES 1

Ingredients

½ measure crème de cassis
4 measures freshly opened chilled champagne

The practice of combining still white wine and black currant liqueur goes back to the 1840s. Lejay-Lagoute, the Dijon distilling house, created crème de cassis in 1841 and, not long after, they added it to wine, giving birth to "blanc cassis," available as a premixed beverage.

The legend of how this drink became known as "Kir," however, is as follows: a priest from Burgundy, going by the name of Canon Félix Kir, realized that by adding crème de cassis to the poor-quality wartime wine, the wine would become more palatable. When he then led a rescue party to recover some wine stolen by German soldiers, he became a hero of the Resistance and thus this drink became known as "Kir" in his honor. The popular "Kir Royale" is the drink created when you substitute champagne for the white wine. There are many other variations besides, such as using other fruit liqueurs or even red wine instead of white, in order to make a "Cardinal."

Method

Pour the crème de cassis into a champagne flute and top off with the freshly opened champagne. Stir lightly, then serve immediately.

ALTERNATIVE A Kir Royale is often served with a whole strawberry in the glass. After adding the crème de cassis, simply add the lightly rinsed strawberry, then top off with the champagne, stir lightly, and serve. This is an ideal drink for a romantic occasion or for Valentine's Day.

Classic Champagne Cocktail

SERVES 1

The origin of this cocktail remains a mystery, but it is thought to have been created around 1850 in the South. In 1888, a cocktail competition was organized by a journalist and the winner was a John Doherty who produced this recipe, which he claimed came from a southern state.

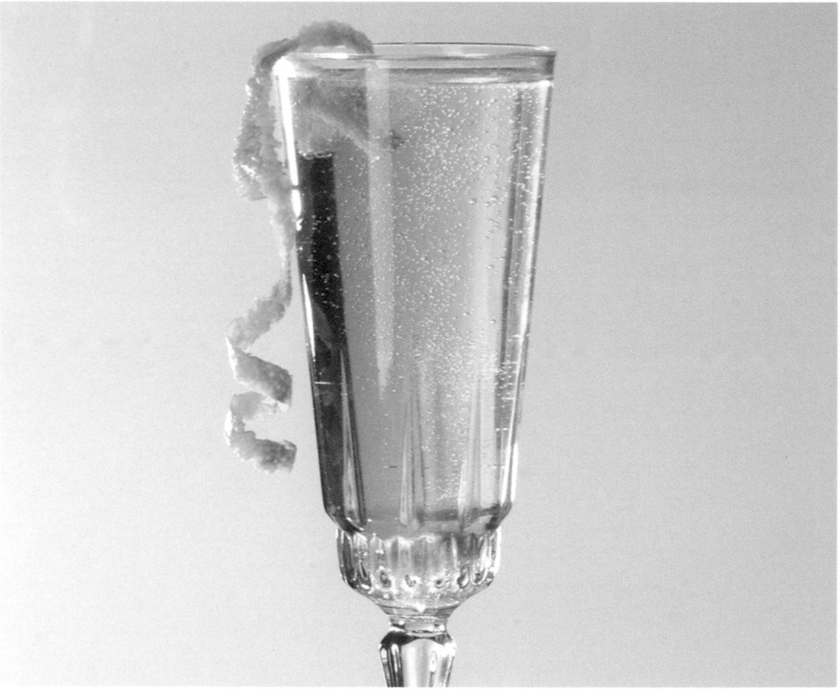

Ingredients

1 sugar cube
2 dashes Angostura bitters
3 measures freshly opened chilled champagne
½ measure cognac
orange twist, to decorate

Method

Place the sugar cube in a champagne flute and shake the Angostura bitters bottle over the sugar cube. Pour in the champagne and cognac, stir lightly, then serve decorated with an orange twist. Serve immediately.

ALTERNATIVE If liked, add a squeeze of lemon or orange before adding the champagne and cognac. Use the same fruit that has been squeezed into the cocktail to decorate.

Great Idea

SERVES 1

Ingredients

1 measure pineapple juice
1 measure mandarin juice
½ measure maple syrup
3 measures freshly opened chilled Champagne
1 small pineapple wedge, to decorate

Method

Pour the pineapple and mandarin juices into a champagne flute and add the maple syrup. Stir with a swizzle stick until the syrup has dissolved in the juice. Carefully pour in the chilled Champagne and serve decorated with a small pineapple wedge.

"Champagne" with a capital C is used to describe a high-quality, sparkling white wine produced in the Champagne area of France. Normally produced by small growers, who then sell their grapes to the Champagne houses of France, only wine that has been made from grapes grown in this area can be called Champagne.

ALTERNATIVE If liked, cava (a sparkling wine from Spain), *méthode traditionelle* sparkling wine (champagne-style wine that is not from the Champagne region), or New World sparkling wines can be used instead of Champagne.

Mimosa

SERVES 1

There are a few recipes for different-flavor Mimosas, none of which is as well known as this classic recipe. Also called a Buck's Fizz, "Buck" refers to the fact that the ingredients have been poured directly into a chilled tall glass and does not necessarily contain Champagne.

Ingredients

2 measures freshly squeezed orange juice
4 measures chilled and freshly opened Champagne
orange twist, to decorate

Method

Pour the orange juice into a champagne flute and top off with the chilled Champagne. Stir lightly with a swizzle stick, then serve immediately, decorated with an orange twist.

ALTERNATIVE For a nonalcoholic version of this drink, use 3 measures freshly squeezed juice from blood oranges, if available, with sparkling elderflower pressé and decorate with either a fresh strawberry or an orange twist.

Black Velvet

SERVES 1

Ingredients

4 measures Guinness
4 measures freshly opened chilled Champagne

Method

Pour the Guinness into a champagne flute and top off with the chilled Champagne. Serve immediately.

This cocktail was created in London around the time that Prince Albert died—1861. The story is that a royal steward decided that, as the whole country was in mourning, so should Champagne be, so he created this cocktail, which became very popular with both royal and commoner alike.

ALTERNATIVE Replace the Guinness with lager, using equal quantities of lager and Champagne. This is then a Halsted Street Velvet.

Tall Black Russian

SERVES 1

Kahlúa is a coffee liqueur made from the finest Mexican coffee beans, cane liquour, and a hint of vanilla. It also contains vodka and is sweetened with cane sugar. The addition of cola makes this drink a tall, sparkling version of the simpler classic Black Russian.

Ingredients

4 ice cubes, crushed
1½ measures vodka
1 measure Kahlúa
4 measures chilled cola
lemon spiral, to decorate

Method

Place the ice cubes in a tall chilled glass, pour in the vodka, then the Kahlúa, and slowly stir in the chilled cola. Serve immediately, decorated with a lemon spiral.

ALTERNATIVE Try using a chocolate stick as a swizzle stick for added sweetness and flavor.

New Orleans

SERVES 1

Ingredients

3 ice cubes
1 measure white rum
½ measure peach brandy
1 tsp. freshly squeezed orange juice
freshly opened chilled Champagne

Method

Place the ice in a cocktail shaker and add the rum, peach brandy, and orange juice. Shake for 30 seconds, then pour into a champagne flute, top off with Champagne, and serve.

When beginning to make cocktails, perhaps one of the most important things to remember is to measure accurately and not to add more than is stated. If you do, you may find that, not only does the drink become unpalatable due to an overriding taste, it could have the effect of making your guest drunk too quickly—thus ending a party more quickly than anticipated.

ALTERNATIVE Replace the white rum with bourbon, the peach brandy with Pernod, and add a dash of Angostura bitters. Stir in a little sugar to taste and decorate with a twist of lemon zest.

Bellini

SERVES 1

Ingredients

2 measures vodka
½ measure peach schnapps
1 tsp. peach juice
freshly opened chilled Champagne
peach slice, to decorate

The Bellini was first invented by one Giuseppe Cipriani, owner of Harry's Bar, Venice, in the 1930s or 1940s. It is one of Italy's most popular cocktails and is traditionally made with that country's fine sparkling wine, Prosecco, although Champagne or other sparkling wine is often used. The recipe we provide here suggests adding a little kick with vodka and peach schnapps, but, if you were to make a strictly traditional Bellini, you would have to use just Prosecco and fresh white-peach puree.

To achieve the authentic look of the original Bellini, you could add a dash of raspberry or cherry juice to give the drink a pink glow—although this is not part of the standard IBA (International Bartenders Association) recipe. The pink glow of Cipriani's original concoction apparently reminded him of the color of the toga of a saint in a painting by fifteenth-century Venetian artist Giovanni Bellini and thus inspired him in his choice of name.

Method

Pour the vodka, peach schnapps, and peach juice into a cocktail shaker and shake for 20 seconds. Pour into a chilled champagne flute, then top off with the chilled champagne. Serve immediately, decorated with the peach slice.

ALTERNATIVE Use pureed peach instead of schnapps and peach juice, for a slightly thicker, less alcoholic drink.

Disaronno Mimosa

SERVES 1

Ingredients

½ measure Amaretto Disaronno
2 measures freshly squeezed orange juice, strained
2 measures freshly opened chilled Champagne
orange twist, to decorate

Method

Pour the Amaretto Disaronno and then the strained orange juice into a champagne flute. Stir, then top off with the Champagne and decorate with the orange twist. Serve immediately.

When choosing the Champagne to use in a cocktail, choose carefully. Do not be tempted just because it is going to be mixed with a liquor, liqueur, or fruit juice to buy the cheapest possible—this will certainly affect the taste. However, do not use the most expensive, because that is just a waste. Choose a middle-of-the-road bottle and make sure that it is well chilled and opened only when required.

ALTERNATIVE Try using chilled pink Champagne for this cocktail, especially if serving for a celebration.

Cherry Champagne

SERVES 1

Maraschino cherries were originally produced for royalty and the wealthy and were considered a great delicacy. The cherries are preserved in brine, drained, and steeped in alcohol, and finally sweetened in a syrup that has the addition of food coloring. The red maraschino cherries are flavored with almond, while the green colored cherries are flavored with peppermint.

Ingredients

2 ice cubes, crushed
½ measure cherry brandy
4 measures freshly opened chilled Champagne
3–4 maraschino cherries, to decorate

Method

Place the ice cubes in a champagne flute and pour over the cherry brandy. Top off with the chilled Champagne and serve decorated with the cherries threaded onto a toothpick and placed across the rim of the glass.

ALTERNATIVE Try replacing the cherry brandy with 1 measure kirsch and add 2 teaspoons of the syrup from the jar of maraschino cherries.

Champagne Charlie

SERVES 1

Ingredients

2–3 ice cubes, crushed
1 measure apricot brandy
4 measures freshly opened chilled champagne
1 rose petal or orange twist, to decorate

Method

Place the crushed ice in a Champagne flute and pour in the apricot brandy. Top up with the chilled Champagne and serve decorated with the rose petal floating on top, or an orange twist.

This cocktail is named after the founder and owner of the very famous Champagne house, Heidsieck, which started producing Champagne in 1851. His skills as a salesman and his good-time image earned him the name "Champagne Charlie."

ALTERNATIVE Replace the apricot brandy with a good-quality Calvados and decorate the champagne flute with an apple wedge.

Champagne Napoleon

SERVES 1

Ingredients

2 ice cubes
½ measure Mandarine Napoléon
1 measure freshly squeezed and strained orange juice
4 measures freshly opened chilled Champagne
orange twist and 1 maraschino cherry, to decorate

Method

Place the ice cubes in a cocktail shaker and add the Mandarine Napoléon and the strained orange juice. Shake for 20 seconds, then pour into a champagne flute and top off with Champagne. Decorate with an orange twist and a cherry.

It is said that, on the eve of battle in 1814, Napoleon was explaining his battle plans to Monsieur Moët and it is reputed he said, "In case I fail, I wish to reward you for the way you have conducted your business"—and with that, he took off from his uniform jacket the Chevalier Cross of the Legion of Honor, which he promptly gave to Monsieur Moët.

ALTERNATIVE Briefly stir the ingredients, instead of shaking, before topping off with the Champagne.

Horn of Plenty

SERVES 1

Ingredients

2 ice cubes, crushed
1 measure Grand Marnier
½ measure Campari
½ measure grenadine
3 measures freshly opened chilled Champagne

Method

Place the crushed ice in a champagne flute and pour in the Grand Marnier, Campari, and grenadine. Stir to mix, then top off with the chilled Champagne and serve.

Grand Marnier is similar to triple sec because it is a blend of cognac, distilled extract of orange and other undisclosed ingredients and was created in 1880 by Alexandre Marnier-Lapostolle. It has a 40-percent alcohol content.

ALTERNATIVE Cava or sparkling wine can be used in place of the Champagne, if liked.

Henry's Special

SERVES 1

Ingredients

2 ice cubes
½ measure brandy
1 measure freshly squeezed grapefruit juice
1 tsp. freshly squeezed lemon juice
1 level tsp. honey
3 measures freshly opened chilled Champagne
long cinnamon stick, to use as a stirrer

Method

Place the ice in a cocktail shaker and add the brandy, grapefruit juice, lemon juice, and honey. Shake for 20–30 seconds until well blended. Strain into a champagne flute and top off with the chilled Champagne. Serve with the cinnamon stick to use as a stirrer.

Once Champagne or any sparkling wine, such as cava, has been opened, it quickly loses its fizz. If you do not use all the bottle, try this way of keeping the fizz in: place a teaspoon, bowl end uppermost, in the open bottle. Store in the refrigerator. This will keep the bubbles in the wine for up to 24 hours.

ALTERNATIVE If liked, gently warm the honey before adding to the shaker and place the crushed ice directly into the chilled champagne flute. This will make the drink slightly sweeter.

Night & Day

SERVES 1

Campari is an alcoholic apéritif that is an infusion of bitter herbs with aromatic plants and fruits, which are then steeped in alcohol. The red color comes from cochineal. It is classified as a "bitter." As with many of the liqueurs, it originated in Italy and the original secret recipe is still used to this day.

Ingredients

1 measure cognac
½ measure Grand Marnier
½ measure Campari
2 ice cubes, crushed
3 measures freshly opened chilled Champagne
fresh strawberry, to decorate

Method

Pour the cognac with the Grand Marnier and Campari into a cocktail shaker and shake for 30 seconds, or until blended. Place the crushed ice in a champagne flute and pour over the cognac mixture. Top off with the chilled Champagne and serve decorated with the strawberry.

ALTERNATIVE Replace the cognac with a fruit-flavor brandy.

Snowball

SERVES 1

Ingredients

3 ice cubes
2 measures advocaat
½ measure freshly squeezed and strained lime juice (or use lime syrup)
5 measures lemon-flavor soda
2 maraschino cherries threaded onto a toothpick, to decorate

Method

Place the ice in a glass. Pour over the advocaat and then the lime juice or syrup. Stir, then top off with the soda and serve decorated with the cherries.

This used to be very popular with the ladies in all the trendy drinking spots throughout Europe during the 1960s and fitted in perfectly with the mood of the times. Nowadays, it is still popular in northern Europe. It is a delicious low-alcohol drink, perfect for those who do not want to miss out, but are watching their alcohol intake.

ALTERNATIVE Replace the soda with chilled cava or sparkling wine to give the drink a bit of a kick.

Gagarin

SERVES 1

Named after the USSR's first cosmonaut, this cocktail features vodka, another staple icon of Soviet culture. When serving vodka, many purists state that the liquor should be kept cold at all times, so, with that in mind, vodka is often kept in the freezer.

Ingredients

2 ice cubes
1 measure vodka
½ measure cherry brandy
½ measure crème de cassis
1 tsp. freshly squeezed lemon juice
3 measures dry Babycham
maraschino cherry, to decorate

Method

Place the ice cubes, together with the vodka, cherry brandy, crème de cassis, and lemon juice, into a cocktail shaker. Shake for 30 seconds, or until a frost forms on the outside. Pour into a champagne flute, top off with the Babycham and serve decorated with the maraschino cherry.

ALTERNATIVE Use Champagne or cava in place of the Babycham.

New Orleans Dandy

SERVES 1

Ingredients

3 ice cubes
1 measure white rum
½ measure peach brandy
1 tsp. freshly squeezed orange juice
1 tsp. freshly squeezed lime juice
4–5 measures freshly opened chilled Champagne
orange and lime slices, to decorate

Method

Place the ice cubes in a cocktail shaker and pour in the rum together with the peach brandy and the orange and lime juices. Shake for 20 seconds, then strain into a champagne glass. Top off with the Champagne and serve decorated with orange and lime slices.

Rum is a liquor made from the by-products of sugar cane. The best-known rum is dark rum, but there are various others, such as white rum, which is light-bodied and has a subtle flavor and is usually used as a mixer. Golden rum is more full-bodied with a smooth, mellow taste. There is also spiced rum, which can be white, golden, or dark in color and is infused with fruit spices. Try them, and enjoy.

ALTERNATIVE Try golden rum instead of white. There are many different rums produced in the Caribbean, as each island has its own variety. If not traveling to one of these islands, look in high-quality liquor stores.

White Witch

SERVES 1

Beware of this cocktail: It may look innocent enough being almost pure white in color, but, in fact, its looks belie its effect—it has a hefty kick, even though the taste is pure magic.

Ingredients

4 ice cubes
1–2 measures white rum
½ measure white crème de cacao
½ measure Cointreau
1 tbsp. lime juice
club soda
lime slice, to decorate

Method

Place half the ice cubes in a cocktail shaker with the white rum, crème de cacao, and Cointreau. Add the lime juice, then shake for 30 seconds. Place the remaining ice cubes in an old-fashioned glass (*see* page 30), then strain the cocktail into the glass. Top off with club soda and serve decorated with a lime slice.

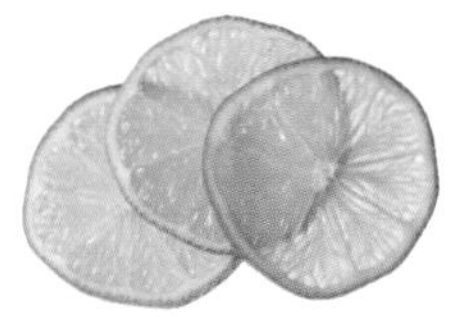

ALTERNATIVE Make a Red Witch cocktail. Simply place crushed ice into a tall glass, add 1 measure Pernod, and 2 measures black currant syrup. Top off with cider and serve.

Bouncing Bomb

SERVES 1

No one is really sure where the name for this cocktail came from. Many believe it was created during the Second World War by American airmen when on leave and relaxing.

Ingredients

4 ice cubes
2 measures brandy
1 measure yellow curaçao
club soda
orange twist, to decorate

Method

Place the ice cubes in a cocktail shaker and add the brandy and curaçao. Shake for 30 seconds. Pour into a highball glass (*see* page 30) and top off with club soda. Decorate with an orange twist and serve.

ALTERNATIVE You can vary the liquor used, so try bourbon, vodka, or gin.

Rum & Guava Fizz

SERVES 2–3

When serving cocktails, a nice touch is to frost the glasses. It is really simple. Place some superfine sugar about ¼ inch thick in a saucer. Dip the rim of the glass into water, orange or lemon juice and then dip immediately into the sugar. Let stand for a few minutes to set before adding the drink.

Ingredients

3 ripe guavas
6 measures rum, preferably white rum
2 measures pineapple juice
crushed ice
½ bottle sparkling white wine

Method

Peel the guavas and discard the seeds. Pass through a juicer into a pitcher, then stir in the rum and pineapple juice. Place some crushed ice in tall glasses, pour over the guava mixture, top off with the sparkling wine, and serve.

ALTERNATIVE Replace the sparkling wine with sparkling apple juice, lemon-flavor soda, or mineral water and use a few dashes Angostura bitters in place of the rum.

Horse's Neck

SERVES 1

Ingredients

3 ice cubes
1½ measures brandy
ginger ale
long lemon zest spiral, to decorate

Method

Place the ice in a glass and pour in the brandy. Top off with the ginger ale, then hang the lemon zest spiral on the glass rim and serve.

This cocktail gets its name from the traditional decoration, which is a long lemon zest spiral that is used to decorate the glass.

ALTERNATIVE The brandy can be replaced with other liquors, if preferred. Try gin, vodka, or whisky.

Gin Sling

SERVES 1

Ingredients

4 ice cubes
2 measures gin
½ measure sugar syrup (*see* page 31)
1 measure freshly squeezed lemon juice
2 measures chilled water, noncarbonated or sparkling, according to taste
pinch freshly grated nutmeg
lemon twist, to decorate

Method

Place the ice in a tall glass and pour over the gin, sugar syrup, and lemon juice. Stir, then top off with the chilled water and serve sprinkled with the freshly grated nutmeg and decorated with the lemon twist.

It is widely believed that "slings" were first created in the United States and the name comes from a German word (*schlock*) meaning "to swallow quickly," the idea being that "you sling the drink down your neck as quickly as possible." Originally, a sling was made using only noncarbonated cold water but, nowadays, a sparkling water is more normal.

ALTERNATIVE Replace the gin with the same amount of brandy, vodka, rum, or bourbon.

John Collins

SERVES 1

Ingredients

4 ice cubes, crushed
2 measures bourbon
1 measure freshly squeezed lemon juice
½ measure sugar syrup
chilled club soda
lemon slice, to decorate

Method

Place the ice cubes in a chilled tall glass, such as a highball glass (*see* page 30), then pour over the bourbon, lemon juice, and sugar syrup. Stir with a swizzle stick, then top off with the club soda, decorate with a lemon slice, and serve.

A Collins is an ideal drink for the hot weather. Normally, it is not shaken but made and served in a tall glass with a liquor, such as bourbon, plus lemon or lime juice and sugar syrup (*see* page 31), and topped off with club soda.

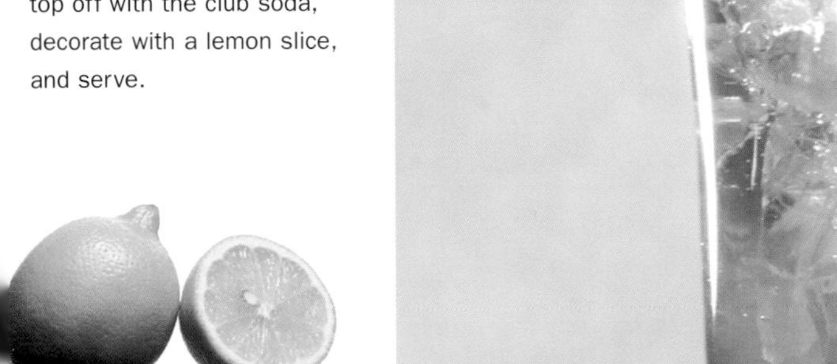

ALTERNATIVE There are many variations to a John Collins. Try a Rum Collins by replacing the bourbon with rum; or a Mint Collins by replacing the bourbon with vodka and adding a measure of crème de menthe.

Tom Collins

SERVES 1

Ingredients

3 ice cubes
2 measures gin
1 measure freshly squeezed lemon juice
½ measure sugar syrup (*see* page 31)
5 measures club soda
lemon or lime twist, to decorate

Method

Place the ice in a tall, chilled highball glass (*see* page 30) and pour in the gin, freshly squeezed lemon juice, and sugar syrup. Stir lightly, then top off with the club soda and serve decorated with the lemon or lime twist.

Originally, this would have been made with “Old Tom Gin,” a gin sold in London when Prohibition was in force. A certain Captain Dudley Bradstreet hung up a sign in the shape of a cat and called it “Old Tom.” The customers would put an amount of money in its mouth and from its paw (via a tube) a measure of gin would flow.

ALTERNATIVE Other “Collins” drinks include a Sandy Collins, with Scotch whisky, and a Brandy Collins.

Apricot Cooler

SERVES 1

Ingredients

4 ice cubes
2 measures apricot brandy
1 measure freshly squeezed lemon juice
1 tsp. grenadine
2–3 dashes Angostura bitters
2 measures club soda
2 measures lemon-flavor soda
lemon zest spiral, to decorate

Method

Place the ice cubes in a collins glass (*see* page 30) and pour in the apricot brandy, lemon juice, grenadine, and Angostura bitters. Stir lightly, then top off with the club soda and lemon-flavor soda. Serve decorated with the lemon zest spiral and add a swizzle stick.

Coolers are prepared in the same manner as a Collins and served in the same kind of glass. They often contain a long spiral or twist of citrus zest and contain any kind of liquor. Normally, they are not shaken unless containing egg white.

ALTERNATIVE For a nonalcoholic version of this cooler, replace the apricot brandy with apricot nectar and the Angostura bitters with a few dashes Worcestershire sauce.

Singapore Sling

SERVES 1

Ingredients

1 measure gin
1 measure cherry brandy
½ measure Bénédictine
½ measure freshly squeezed lime juice
4 measures freshly squeezed orange juice
3 ice cubes, crushed
club soda
small pineapple wedge and a fresh cherry, to decorate

Yet another cocktail whose development is somewhat unclear, the Singapore Sling varies in its recipe. Though it is agreed that Raffles Hotel in Singapore is its birthplace, it seems that the cocktails served there now are not necessarily made to the original recipe. The hotel's Long Bar menu credits Hainanese-Chinese bartender Mr. Ngiam Tong Boon with its creation around the turn of the twentieth century and states that it was originally meant as a woman's drink, "hence the attractive pink color," and that, "Today, it is very definitely a drink enjoyed by all, without which any visit to Raffles Hotel is incomplete."

However, in his Bartender Guide of 1948, Trader Vic quotes the Raffles Hotel Sling as containing just gin, cherry brandy, Bénédictine, soda, and a lime peel decoration, whereas the Singapore Sling as described on the hotel's current menu also contains pineapple juice, lime juice, Cointreau, and Angostura bitters.

Method

Pour the gin, cherry brandy, and Bénédictine into a cocktail shaker. Strain in the lime and orange juices and shake for 30 seconds, or until blended. Place the ice cubes in a collins glass (*see* page 30) and pour over the cocktail. Top off with the club soda, add a swizzle stick, and decorate with the pineapple wedge and a cherry.

ALTERNATIVE Replace the lime juice with lemon juice, the orange juice with mango juice, and use sparkling mineral water in place of the club soda.

Moscow Mule

SERVES 1

Ingredients

3 ice cubes, crushed
2 measures chilled vodka
freshly squeezed juice
 of 2 limes
ginger beer
lime slice, to decorate

Method

Place the crushed ice in a chilled tall glass, such as a highball (*see* page 30), and pour over the vodka, then the freshly squeezed strained lime juice. Stir with a swizzle stick or bar spoon, top off with ginger beer, and serve decorated with a lime slice.

This cocktail was created by John Martin, a liquor distributor. Before 1930, vodka was unknown in this country. After John Martin had bought the rights, he started to market the sale of vodka. Whether by chance or design, he met up with two friends, one who had a glut of ginger beer—hence the Moscow Mule was created.

ALTERNATIVE Try using different flavor vodkas—try cherry, lemon, coconut, chocolate, or even a herb-flavor vodka. Whichever you choose, remember to keep it chilled.

Vodka Twist Fizz

SERVES 1

A fizz is similar to a Collins, but is always shaken before the fizz is added. It normally does not contain very much ice, to avoid inhibiting the fizz of the drink. Serve it in the morning or at midday with a swizzle stick and a straw.

Ingredients

2 ice cubes
2 tbsp. freshly squeezed lime juice
½ tsp. sugar syrup (*see* page 31)
1 large egg white, preferably organic
3 dashes Pernod
3 measures vodka
ginger ale
lime slice, to decorate

Method

Place the ice cubes in a cocktail shaker and strain in the lime juice. Add the sugar syrup with the egg white, Pernod, and vodka. Shake for 45 seconds, or until well blended and a frost starts to form on the outside of the shaker. Pour into a chilled highball glass (*see* page 30) filled halfway with ice and serve topped off with ginger ale and decorated with the lime slice; add a straw and a swizzle stick.

ALTERNATIVE If liked, replace the Pernod and ginger ale with grenadine and club soda and add the freshly squeezed juice from 1 small orange.

Cuba Libre

SERVES 1

It is widely believed this cocktail was created by American soldiers celebrating the end of the Spanish-American War and Cuba's freedom.

Ingredients

1 tbsp. freshly squeezed, strained lime juice
3 ice cubes, crushed
2 measures Bacardi rum
5 measures cola
orange spiral, to decorate

Method

Cut the squeezed lime shell in half and place in a chilled highball glass (*see* page 30). Pour the lime juice into the glass. Spoon in the ice, then pour over the rum and top off with the cola. Add a straw and a swizzle stick and decorate with an orange spiral.

ALTERNATIVE Replace the Bacardi rum with dark rum and use orange juice in place of the lime juice.

French '75

SERVES 1

Ingredients

1 measure gin
1 measure freshly squeezed lemon juice
1 tsp. superfine sugar
4 ice cubes
5 measures freshly opened chilled Champagne
1 maraschino cherry, to decorate

Method

Pour the gin and lemon juice into a chilled collins glass and sprinkle in the sugar. Stir until the sugar has dissolved, then add the ice cubes. Pour in the Champagne and serve with a straw and a maraschino cherry.

The very first "French" was created in Paris during the First World War, and this cocktail takes its name from the French '75 light field gun that was used during the war. French '75s are made in tall glasses, such as a collins (*see* page 30).

ALTERNATIVE Replace the gin with either bourbon or cognac.

Long, Short & Creamy Cocktails

Brandy Alexander

SERVES 1

Allegedly created in 1922 for the wedding of Mary, Princess Royal and Countess of Harewood, and Viscount Lascelles, in London, the Brandy Alexander is the most common cousin of the original gin-based Alexander cocktail around which all the other Alexanders are based.

Ingredients

- 3 ice cubes
- 1 measure brandy
- 1 measure dark crème de cacao
- 1 measure heavy cream
- grated nutmeg, to decorate
- chocolate stick or swizzle stick, to serve

Method

Place the ice in a cocktail shaker and pour in the brandy, crème de cacao and cream. Shake for 30 seconds, or until thoroughly blended, then pour into a short glass. Sprinkle the top with a little freshly grated nutmeg and serve with a chocolate stick or a swizzle stick to stir.

ALTERNATIVE Replace the grated nutmeg with a little grated semisweet chocolate. The brandy can be replaced with white or dark rum or Amaretto liqueur.

Frostbite

SERVES 1

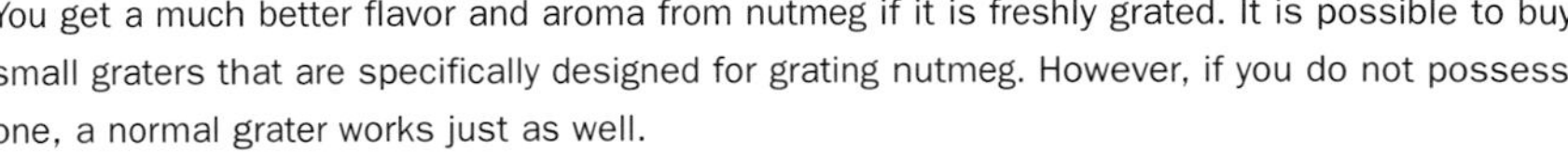

You get a much better flavor and aroma from nutmeg if it is freshly grated. It is possible to buy small graters that are specifically designed for grating nutmeg. However, if you do not possess one, a normal grater works just as well.

Ingredients

3 ice cubes
1 measure tequila
1 measure heavy cream
1 measure white crème de cacao
freshly grated nutmeg, to decorate

Method

Place the ice cubes in a cocktail shaker and add the tequila, heavy cream, and white crème de cacao. Shake for 30 seconds, or until well blended, then strain into a short glass and serve sprinkled with a little freshly grated nutmeg.

ALTERNATIVE Add ½ measure blue curaçao to achieve a more frostbitten effect!

White Russian

SERVES 1

Tia Maria is a coffee liqueur made using Jamaican Blue Mountain coffee beans, which are blended with cane spirit, sugar, and vanilla and allowed to ferment until an alcohol is produced. It can be drunk over ice, by itself, or as part of a cocktail.

Ingredients

4 ice cubes
1 measure vodka
1 measure Tia Maria
1 measure heavy cream
freshly grated chocolate, to decorate

Method

Place 2 ice cubes into a cocktail shaker and add the vodka, Tia Maria, and heavy cream. Shake for 30 seconds, or until well blended. Place the 2 remaining ice cubes in a short glass and strain over the cocktail. Sprinkle the top with the grated chocolate and serve with a straw, if liked.

ALTERNATIVE If preferred, the heavy cream can be replaced with whole milk for a slightly less creamy cocktail.

Angel's Treat

SERVES 1

Ingredients

1 ice cube
1½ measures dark rum
1 measure amaretto liqueur
2 tbsp. whipped cream
2 tsp. finely grated chocolate

Method

Place the ice into a cocktail shaker and add the rum, amaretto, and 1 tablespoon of the whipped cream. Add 1 teaspoon of the grated chocolate, then shake for 30 seconds, or until blended. Strain into a short glass and float the remaining whipped cream on top. Sprinkle with the remaining grated chocolate and serve.

There is no hard and fast rule whether you use milk or semisweet dark chocolate in this cocktail; it is a question of personal taste. The only thing to remember is that, when using chocolate, as with all ingredients, it is always worth using the best you can afford.

ALTERNATIVE Add a measure of crème de cacao to this luscious creamy drink.

Whiskey with a Twist

SERVES 2

Ingredients

1 small melon wedge, such as galia or cantaloupe
1 small orange
5 measures whiskey
4 tbsp. ginger wine
2 tbsp. crushed ice, to serve
2 orange twists, to decorate

Method

Discard the skin and seeds from the melon and cut into chunks. Peel the orange, discarding the bitter white pith, and divide into segments. Place the fruits with the whiskey and ginger wine in a smoothie machine or blender. If using a smoothie machine, blend on mix for 15 seconds and then on smooth for 45 seconds. If using a blender, blend for 1–2 minutes until smooth. Place the crushed ice in glasses. Pour over the whiskey mixture, decorate the glasses with orange twists, and serve.

When using whiskey in a cocktail, use the blended varieties because they offer excellent value for money. Save the malt whiskies to drink by themselves.

ALTERNATIVE Replace the whiskey with more ginger wine.

Alexander's Sister

SERVES 1

Ingredients

4 ice cubes
1 measure dark rum
1 measure Kahlúa
1 measure heavy cream
freshly grated nutmeg
or chocolate

Method

Place the ice cubes into a cocktail shaker and add the rum, Kahlúa, and heavy cream. Shake for 30 seconds, or until well blended, then strain into a cocktail glass and serve decorated with the freshly grated nutmeg or chocolate.

Another cocktail that is based on the Brandy Alexander. This one has a distinct coffee aroma and flavor. As well as sprinkling the top of the cocktail with a little grated chocolate or nutmeg, try frosting the rim of the glass using 1 tablespoon grated chocolate and water. Simply dip the glass in the water and then the chocolate, then let it dry.

ALTERNATIVE There are many variations with Alexanders and one very easy one is to use 1 measure each of brandy, cream, and Kahlúa. Simply shake until blended, then strain into a cocktail glass and serve.

Margarita

SERVES 1

Ingredients

1 measure freshly squeezed lemon juice
1 tbsp. salt
2 measures tequila
1½ measures triple sec
½ measure blue curaçao
½ measure freshly squeezed lemon juice

Stories abound regarding the invention of the margarita, which appears to have been created at some point between the 1930s and the late 1940s, usually involving a woman named "Margarita" or "Majorie." One tale claims how bar owner Danny Negrete presented it to his sister-in-law as a wedding present and named the drink after her. Or is it true that Carlos "Danny" Herrera, a barman at Rancho La Gloria at Rosarito Beach, Mexico, created the drink for showgirl Marjorie King? Marjorie was reportedly allergic to all hard alcohol except tequila, but could not drink it straight; so Danny mixed it up just for her.

Another well-known story is that society hostess Margaret Sames created the drink when experimenting with various concoctions for her guests at her home in Acapulco. Whatever the true origins are, this is a classic cocktail enjoyed by many and which, of course, can vary greatly in its preparation (*see* also page 292).

Method

Using the lemon juice and salt, frost the glass (*see* page 31) and let dry. Place the tequila in a cocktail shaker with the triple sec, blue curaçao, and ½ measure lemon juice. Shake for 30 seconds until blended, pour into the frosted glass, and serve.

ALTERNATIVE Replace the blue curaçao and the triple sec with 1 measure green curaçao or Galliano. To make a Frozen Margarita, fill a glass with crushed ice and pour over the shaken cocktail.

Frozen Fruit Margarita

SERVES 1

Ingredients

1 measure freshly squeezed lemon juice
1 tbsp. superfine sugar
1½ measures tequila
1 measure strawberry liqueur
½ measure triple sec
3 ice cubes, crushed
1 fresh strawberry fan

Method

Using the lemon juice and sugar, frost the glass (*see* page 31) and let dry. Place the tequila in a cocktail shaker with the remaining lemon juice, strawberry liqueur, and triple sec and add the crushed ice. Shake for 30 seconds, or until blended, then pour into the glass and serve decorated with the strawberry fan.

These are really simple to make and provide a delicious fruity drink, absolutely perfect for relaxing and having fun. Try experimenting with your favorite fruits and mixer liqueurs.

ALTERNATIVE Use Midori, Cointreau, or Grand Marnier in place of the strawberry liqueur and decorate with the appropriate fruit.

Bazooka

SERVES 1

Ingredients

1 measure Southern Comfort
½ measure crème de banane
1 tsp. grenadine
2 tbsp. whipped cream
2 ice cubes
banana slice and maraschino cherry, to decorate

Method

Place the Southern Comfort in a cocktail shaker with the crème de banane and grenadine. Add half of the whipped cream and half of the ice and shake for 30 seconds. Place the remaining ice into a short glass and strain over the shaken cocktail. Top off with the remaining whipped cream and serve decorated with the fruit and a stirrer.

Created in New Orleans around 1874, Southern Comfort was the result of a bartender, Wilkes Heron, wanting to improve the flavor of the harsh local brandy. He started adding other liquors as well as spices and other flavors. After much experimentation, Southern Comfort was born; its recipe remains to this day a closely guarded secret.

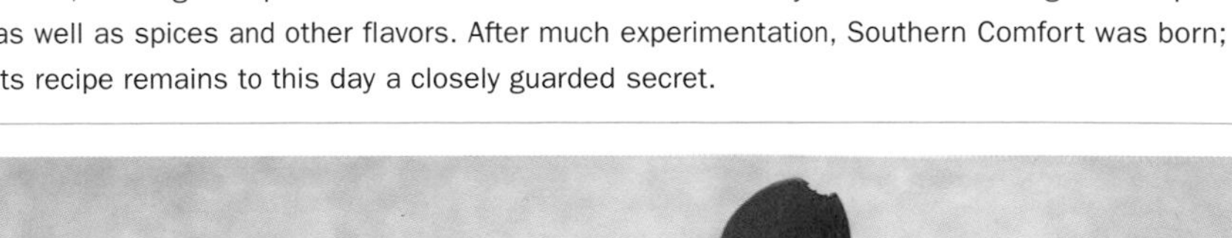

ALTERNATIVE Replace the Southern Comfort with white rum and sprinkle the whipped cream floating on top with a little grated chocolate.

Caribbean Sunset

SERVES 1

Ingredients

3 ice cubes
1 measure crème de banane
½ measure blue curaçao
½ measure freshly squeezed lemon juice
½ measure mango juice
2 tbsp. whipped cream
1 tsp. grenadine
star fruit (carambola) slice and small mango wedge, or halved strawberry, to decorate

Method

Place a couple of the ice cubes in a cocktail shaker and the remaining ice into a short glass. Pour the crème de banane into the cocktail shaker together with the blue curaçao, the lemon and mango juices, and half the whipped cream. Shake for 30 seconds, or until blended. Pour over the ice and add the grenadine, letting it sink slowly. Top with the remaining cream, decorate, and serve.

This cocktail is so named because the colors reflect not only the glorious sunsets in the Caribbean, but the flavor and aromas from the Islands.

ALTERNATIVE Try adding ½ measure gin for more bite.

Tropical Bubbles

SERVES 2

This delicious drink is crammed full of ripe, plump Caribbean fruits. For maximum flavor, chill the fruits for a short while before using.

Ingredients

1 large, ripe mango
1 large, ripe papaya
2 ripe guavas
6 measures pineapple juice
½ bottle chilled Champagne or sparkling wine
mint sprigs, to decorate (optional)
2 pineapple wedges, to decorate (optional)

Method

Peel the mango, papaya, and guavas and discard the pits and seeds. Cut into chunks. Place in a blender and add the pineapple juice. Blend for 1–2 minutes until smooth, then pour into chilled tall glasses and top off with Champagne. Serve with a stirrer, if liked, and decorate with mint sprigs and pineapple wedges.

ALTERNATIVE For a nonalcoholic version, omit the Champagne and use sparkling spring water.

Calvados Cream

SERVES 1

Calvados is an apple brandy that is made in Normandy, France, using fermented apple juice, which is distilled and aged in oak casks. It is used in drinks and can be used in cooking.

Ingredients

2 measures Calvados brandy
½ measure freshly squeezed lemon juice
1 tbsp. fresh organic egg white
2 tbsp. heavy cream
1 tsp. pineapple or sugar syrup (*see* page 31)
2 ice cubes, crushed (optional)
red apple slice, to decorate

Method

Pour the Calvados brandy into a cocktail shaker together with the lemon juice, egg white, cream, and pineapple or sugar syrup. Shake for 30 seconds, or until blended. Place the crushed ice, if using, in a short glass, then pour the cocktail and serve decorated with the apple slice.

ALTERNATIVE Use other brandies and decorations in place of the Calvados, such as apricot brandy, decorated with an apricot slice, or a cherry brandy with a fresh or maraschino cherry as decoration.

Girl Scout

SERVES 1

Ingredients

½ measure schnapps
1 measure white crème de cacao
½ measure Baileys Irish Cream
1 tsp. green crème de menthe
1 tbsp. whipping cream
2 ice cubes, crushed
mint sprig, to decorate

Method

Place the schnapps into a cocktail shaker and add the crème de cacao, Baileys, and crème de menthe. Add the whipping cream and shake for 20 seconds, or until blended. Place the crushed ice in a short glass and pour over the cocktail. Decorate with the mint sprig and serve.

Baileys was the first Irish cream liqueur. It is a blend of Irish whiskey and cream and was introduced to the market in 1974. Although it contains no preservatives, it has a shelf life of 2 years from the date of manufacturing but, once opened, should be used within six months.

ALTERNATIVE Use a thin peppermint chocolate to add that little extra to this fun drink.

Mohican

SERVES 1

Ingredients

1½ measures white crème de cacao
1 measure bourbon
½ measure dry vermouth
1 measure whipping cream
2 ice cubes
½ tsp. freshly grated semisweet dark chocolate

Method

Frost the glass with the chocolate (*see* page 31) and let dry. Place the white crème de cacao in a cocktail shaker and add the bourbon, dry vermouth, and whipping cream. Add the ice and shake for 30 seconds, or until blended. Strain into a cocktail glass (*see* page 29).

One of the best-known bourbons is from Kentucky—and goes under the colorful name of Wild Turkey. Bourbon is an American variation of whiskey and is to Americans what Scotch whisky is to Scotland and Irish whiskey is to Ireland, all firmly stating that theirs is best.

ALTERNATIVE Use one of the other whiskies available—try Canadian rye whiskey or Irish whiskey and taste the difference.

Southern Peach

SERVES 1

Ingredients

1½ measures Southern Comfort
1½ measures peach brandy
1½ measures heavy cream
2 dashes Angostura bitters
1 ice cube, crushed (optional)
peach slices, to decorate

Method

Place the Southern Comfort in a cocktail shaker and add the peach brandy and heavy cream. Add the Angostura bitters and crushed ice, if using. Pour into a cocktail glass, decorate with the peach slices and serve.

This cocktail comes from the Deep South and was created by Wilkes Heron of New Orleans, who was responsible for developing Southern Comfort. This cocktail is one of the many that resulted from his trouble.

ALTERNATIVE If liked, orange bitters can be used in place of the Angostura bitters and the brandy could be replaced with Grand Marnier.

Orange Blossom

SERVES 1

Ingredients

1 measure gin
1½ measures freshly squeezed orange juice
1 measure sweet rosso vermouth
1 ice cube
1 tsp. orange blossom honey or superfine sugar
orange spiral, to decorate

Method

Pour the gin, orange juice, and sweet vermouth into a cocktail shaker and add the ice cube and orange blossom honey or sugar. Shake for 30 seconds, or until blended, then pour into a cocktail glass, decorate with the orange spiral, and serve.

Gin is distilled from nonmalted grain and the resulting spirit is flavored with juniper berries and herbs. One of the largest areas for the growing of juniper berries is Umbria in Italy. It is mainly these berries that give gin its delicate aromatic flavor.

ALTERNATIVE Replace the gin with peach brandy and decorate with peach slices to make a Peach Blossom.

Acapulco

SERVES 1

Ingredients

4 ice cubes, crushed
1 measure tequila
1 measure white rum
2 measures pineapple juice
1 measure freshly squeezed grapefruit juice
1 measure coconut milk
pineapple wedges, to decorate

Method

Place the ice cubes in a cocktail shaker and add the tequila, white rum, and pineapple and grapefruit juices with the coconut milk. Shake for 30 seconds, then pour into a tall glass and serve decorated with pineapple wedges.

This drink was originally made with dark rum, but, due to travelers experiencing the delights of tequila in Mexico and other South American countries, tequila is instead the key ingredient.

ALTERNATIVE If you enjoyed this cocktail, try this variation: 1 measure white rum, 1 measure triple sec, 2 measures strained lime juice, 1 tablespoon sugar, or to taste, and 1 small egg white. Place all the ingredients in a cocktail shaker, shake, and pour over crushed ice. Decorate with a lime wedge and mint sprig.

Piña Colada

SERVES 1

Ingredients

4 ice cubes, crushed
1 measure white rum
2 measures cream of coconut
2 measures pineapple juice
pineapple wedge and maraschino cherry, to decorate

The Piña Colada is known as a Puerto Rican cocktail and there are many who hail from that Caribbean island who lay claim to its invention—such as Ramon "Monchito" Marrero of the Caribe Hilton Hotel, who supposedly invented it in 1954 after much experimentation. However, although it is fair to say that the Piña Colada is inextricably tied to Puerto Rico, it seems that a drink going by that name—which literally means "strained pineapple" in Spanish—was being made much earlier, in Cuba. Originally, it was simply a pineapple juice beverage with ice and sugar, which then evolved to contain rum—according to *Travel* magazine in 1922, the pineapple was "rapidly shaken up with ice, sugar, lime, and Bacardi rum in delicate proportions"—and eventually, somewhere along the line, cream of coconut. Do make sure that, if using fresh pineapple juice, the fruit used is very fresh and perfectly ripe. When served, the whole drink should be milky white with no hint of separation.

Method

Place the crushed ice in a cocktail shaker and pour in the white rum, cream of coconut, and pineapple juice. Shake for 20 seconds, or until well blended. Strain into a tall glass and decorate with the pineapple wedge and cherry and serve with a straw.

ALTERNATIVE Make a "Chi Chi," the Hawaiian version of the Piña Colada, by substituting vodka for the rum.

Egg Nog

SERVES 1

Originally, the word "nog" referred to a strong beer that was brewed in East Anglia in England. It was combined with egg and milk and drunk as a nourishing drink, but was more like a medicine, because it was quite unpalatable. Over the years, it has developed and is now very palatable—the beer has been replaced with brandy.

Ingredients

4 ice cubes
1 very fresh organic egg
1 tbsp. sugar syrup (*see* page 31)
2 measures brandy
6 measures milk
freshly grated nutmeg, to decorate

Method

Place the ice cubes into a cocktail shaker and add the egg, sugar syrup, brandy, and milk. Shake for about 1 minute until well blended, then strain into a tall glass and serve sprinkled with freshly grated nutmeg.

ALTERNATIVE It is a question of personal choice as to which milk you use. If using whole milk, the drink will be creamier than if you use either low-fat or skim milk.

Las Vegas

SERVES 1

Ingredients

3 ice cubes
1 measure tequila
2 measures cream of coconut
2 measures freshly squeezed orange juice
2 measures pineapple juice
1 measure whipped cream
pineapple wedge and maraschino cherry, to decorate

Method

Place the ice in a cocktail shaker and pour in the tequila, cream of coconut, and orange and pineapple juices together with the cream. Shake for 20 seconds, then strain into a tall glass and serve decorated with a pineapple wedge and a cherry. Add a straw, if liked.

There are many myths and mysteries surrounding tequila, including that the drink was originally drunk only by bandits. However, tequila is now enjoyed by all. Even the name is surrounded in mystery; it is said that it is an ancient Nahuatl term meaning "the place of harvesting plants," but one thing is certain—it is a welcome addition to any bar.

ALTERNATIVE Replace the tequila with white rum and use tropical fruit juice in place of the pineapple juice.

Mai Tai

SERVES 1

Ingredients

lightly whisked egg white
1 tbsp. superfine sugar
3 ice cubes, crushed
1½–2 measures dark rum
1 measure clear or orange curaçao
½ measure grenadine
½ measure freshly squeezed orange juice
½ measure freshly squeezed lime juice
orange slice and pineapple wedge, to decorate

Generally accepted to be the invention of the famous Victor J. Bergeron of Trader Vic's Polynesian-style bar in Oakland, California, the Mai Tai is a classic tropical cocktail. Trader Vic reportedly chose the name after some Tahitian friends of his tasted the drink and exclaimed "mai tai roa ae"—"out of this world!" Many variations have been used over the years, but the original recipe seems to have contained 80-percent-proof J. Wray & Nephew rum over shaved ice, with the juice from half a fresh lime, some orange curaçao, a dash of rock candy syrup, and a dollop of French orgeat. You can also use grenadine to get the orange color. The drink is strong and fresh and should not be too watered down with assorted juices.

Perhaps a key point, as made by journalist Rick Carroll, and which applies to all tropical drinks, is that it "always tastes better in a thatch hut on a lagoon with coco palms lining the shore. A great Mai Tai in the Tonga Room of San Francisco's Fairmont Hotel is not the same as a great Mai Tai on Waikiki Beach."

Method

Using the egg white and superfine sugar, frost the glass (*see* page 31) and, once set, carefully fill with the crushed ice. Pour the rum with the curaçao, grenadine, and fruit juices into a cocktail shaker and shake for 30 seconds. Strain carefully over the crushed ice and serve decorated with the orange slice and pineapple wedge.

ALTERNATIVE Use white rum in place of the dark rum and Cointreau instead of curaçao and decorate with a lime twist.

Pineapple Velvet

SERVES 1

Ingredients

5 measures lager, chilled
2 measures pineapple juice, chilled
5 measures Champagne, chilled
small pineapple wedge, to decorate
mint sprig, to decorate (optional)

Method

Pour the lager into a glass, add the pineapple juice, and stir. Top off with the Champagne, decorate with a pineapple wedge and a mint sprig, and serve.

When choosing glasses for cocktails, there are many different varieties. Traditional cocktail glasses contain ⅔ cup and are normally triangular in shape. Of course, if it is a Champagne cocktail being served, as here, then a champagne flute is the perfect glass.

ALTERNATIVE Use ginger beer in place of the lager and sparkling wine in place of the Champagne. Stir and serve with a small pineapple wedge.

Frozen Key Lime

SERVES 1

Ingredients

3 ice cubes
1 measure white rum
½ measure dark rum
1½ measures freshly squeezed lime juice
club soda
1–2 scoops good-quality vanilla ice cream
little grated chocolate, to decorate

Method

Place the ice in a cocktail shaker and pour in the white and dark rums together with the lime juice. Shake for 30 seconds, or until blended, then strain into a tall glass and top off with the club soda. Float the ice cream on top. Sprinkle with the grated chocolate. Serve with a straw and spoon, if liked.

This could almost be regarded as a cross between a dessert and a drink, because it is based on the very popular dessert—Key Lime Pie. Beware, the dessert does not have a kick like this has. Enjoy.

ALTERNATIVE Use a mixture of citrus fruit juices instead of the lime juice and decorate with a twist from each.

Tobago Fizz

SERVES 1

When using citrus fruits for their juice, there are a couple of tricks that are both quick and easy that will help to get the maximum amount of juice from the fruits. Either roll the fruit on a counter for a couple of minutes before attempting to squeeze, or heat for 30–40 seconds in a microwave, cool, then squeeze. Either way, you will get far more juice from the fruits.

Ingredients

4 ice cubes
1 tbsp. freshly squeezed lime juice
2 tbsp. freshly squeezed orange juice
3 measures golden or white rum
1 measure light cream
½ tsp. honey
club soda, to top off
strawberry, to decorate

Method

Place the ice cubes in a cocktail shaker and pour in the lime and orange juices. Add the rum with the cream and honey. Shake for 45 seconds, or until a frost forms on the outside of the cocktail shaker. Strain into a tall glass, top off with club soda, and serve decorated with a strawberry.

ALTERNATIVE For an extra kick, replace the club soda with sparkling wine.

Florida Keys

SERVES 1

Ingredients

4 ice cubes, crushed
2 measures white rum
1 measure freshly squeezed lime juice
1 ripe passion fruit
1 measure heavy cream
orange slice, to decorate

Method

Place the ice cubes in a cocktail shaker and add the white rum and lime juice. Scoop out the pulp and seeds with the juice from the passion fruit and add to the shaker together with the heavy cream. Shake for 45 seconds, or until a frost forms on the outside of the shaker. Pour into a hurricane glass (*see* page 29) and decorate with the orange slice.

Passion fruits are ready for use once they are very wrinkled and the outside skin has begun to cave in. It is not worth using them before, because the flavor and aroma will not have developed.

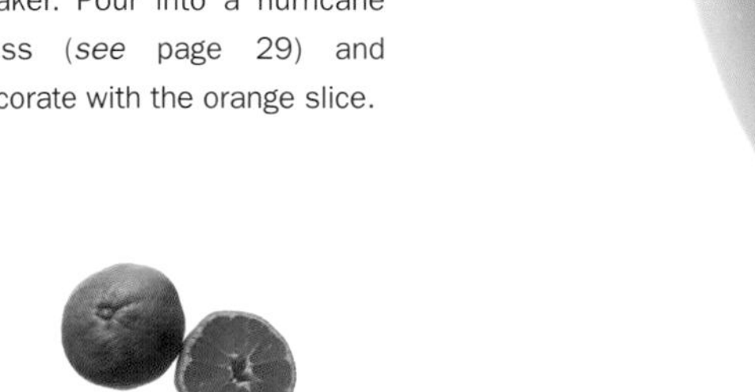

ALTERNATIVE Replace the lime juice and passion fruit with all orange juice. Use 2½ measures freshly squeezed orange juice and strain into the glass.

Long Island Iced Tea

SERVES 1

A hangover is almost guaranteed with just one of these cocktails. It dates back to Prohibition and was originally made with any liquor that was available at that time, which most probably accounts for all the different recipes that are around.

Ingredients

4–6 ice cubes
½ measure white rum
½ measure vodka
½ measure gin
½ measure tequila
½ measure Cointreau
½ measure triple sec
1 measure freshly squeezed lime juice
½ measure sugar syrup (*see* page 31)
4 measures cola
orange twist, to decorate

Method

Place the ice cubes in a tall glass and pour in the rum, vodka, gin, tequila, Cointreau, and triple sec. Stir with a bar spoon, then add the lime juice and sugar syrup and top off with the cola. Serve with a stirrer and decorate with the orange twist.

ALTERNATIVE If liked, omit the tequila and triple sec and add 1 measure blue curaçao.

Cocobanana

SERVES 1

Ingredients

3 ice cubes
1 measure white rum
1 measure crème de banane
½ measure amaretto liqueur
1–1½ measures coconut rum
3 measures pineapple juice
1 measure cream of coconut
½ ripe banana
2 scoops good-quality vanilla ice cream
maraschino cherry, pineapple wedge, and banana slice, to decorate

Method

Place the ice into a cocktail shaker, then pour in the white rum, crème de banane, amaretto, coconut rum, pineapple juice, and cream of coconut. Mash the banana and add to the cocktail shaker together with the ice cream. Shake for 1 minute, or until blended, then pour into a tall glass and serve with a spoon and straw and decorate with the fruit.

This delicious exotic cocktail takes its name from where it originated and, of course, the ingredients used. A perfect cocktail to enjoy when the weather is hot and sunny and the going is tough. It is the ideal way to wind down and chill out.

ALTERNATIVE If liked, place the ingredients into a blender and blend for 20 seconds before straining into the glass.

Passion Fruit & Vodka Smoothie

SERVES 2

Ingredients

2 ripe passion fruits
1 large orange
1–2 tsp. honey, or to taste
6 measures coconut milk
⅔ cup live plain yogurt
5 measures vodka
6 ice cubes
orange wedges, to decorate (optional)

Method

Cut the passion fruits in half and scoop out the flesh and seeds. Strain the fruit if a smoother texture is preferred and reserve the juice. Peel the orange, discarding the bitter white pith, and divide into segments. Place all the ingredients, including the ice cubes, into a smoothie machine or blender. If using a smoothie machine, blend on mix for 10 seconds and then on smooth for 30 seconds. If using a blender, blend for 1–2 minutes until smooth. Pour into glasses, decorate, and serve.

Vodka does not have much, if any, flavor and takes on the flavors that it is blended with. Here, the vodka has been teamed with passion fruit and orange to create a refreshing smoothie with a bit of a kick.

ALTERNATIVE For a nonalcoholic smoothie, replace the vodka with ginger ale or ginger beer and stir in after blending the other ingredients.

Chocolate Monkey

SERVES 1

Ingredients

1 tbsp. finely grated semisweet chocolate
3 ice cubes, crushed
1 measure crème de banane
1 measure white rum
½ –1 measure chocolate syrup
½ ripe banana
2 tbsp. heavy cream, lightly whipped
banana slices and strawberry, to decorate

Method

Frost the glass (*see* page 31) with the chocolate and let dry. Place the crushed ice in a blender with the crème de banane, rum, and chocolate syrup. Slice the banana and add to the blender. Blend for 20–30 seconds, then pour into a tall glass and float the cream on top. Sprinkle the top with grated chocolate to taste, serve with a straw and spoon, and decorate with the fruit.

This cocktail is definitely for the chocoholics and, if liked, you can increase the amount of chocolate used. Chocolate and rum are the perfect combination and, when cream is added, the result is sublime.

ALTERNATIVE Use a cocktail shaker, if liked. Simply place all the ingredients in the shaker and shake for 45 seconds, or until blended. Pour into the glass, float with the cream, decorate, and serve.

Island Affair

SERVES 1

Ingredients

3 ice cubes, crushed
1 measure Midori
(melon liqueur)
1–1½ measures Cointreau
½ measure blue curaçao
1½ measures freshly
squeezed orange juice
2 measures mango juice
1 tbsp. lightly whipped cream
mango slice, pineapple
slice, and melon wedge,
to decorate

Method

Place the crushed ice in a tall glass. Pour the Midori into a cocktail shaker, together with the Cointreau, blue curaçao, and the fruit juices. Shake for 30 seconds, or until blended, then strain over the crushed ice. Float the whipped cream on top and serve with a straw and spoon and decorate with the fruits.

Mango is a large tropical fruit that is growing in popularity throughout the world. It does need to be eaten when ripe, otherwise the delicious flavor will not have developed. Let ripen at room temperature before using and, once ripe, store in the vegetable compartment of the refrigerator, but let it reach room temperature before using.

ALTERNATIVE If mango juice is not available, use well-drained canned mango instead.

Lazy Daze

SERVES 1

Ingredients

3 ice cubes, crushed
1 measure vodka
1 measure Kahlúa
½ measure green crème de menthe
2 measures lemon-flavor soda
1 tbsp. whipped cream
mint sprig, to decorate

Method

Place the crushed ice in a tall glass. Pour the vodka into a cocktail shaker with the Kahlúa liqueur and crème de menthe. Shake for 20 seconds, then pour into the ice-filled glass. Top off with the soda. Float the cream on top and decorate with a mint sprig.

Crème de menthe is a peppermint- or spearmint-flavored liqueur and is available either green or clear (referred to as white). Both varieties are interchangeable unless the color is crucial to the finished drink or dish. It can be served over ice as a *digestif* or combined with other ingredients to give a refreshing hint of mint. In some instances, it is also added to food.

ALTERNATIVE Kahlúa is a coffee liqueur. If unavailable, use 1 measure strong coffee with 1 measure brandy.

Love in the Afternoon

SERVES 1

Ingredients

2 measures dark rum
½ measure strawberry liqueur
1 measure freshly squeezed orange juice
½ measure cream of coconut
2 tsp. sugar syrup (*see* page 31)
crushed ice
4 ripe strawberries, lightly rinsed

Method

Place the rum with the strawberry liqueur, orange juice, cream of coconut, and sugar syrup into a blender. Reserve 1 of the strawberries to use as decoration, slice the remainder, and add to the blender. Blend for 20 seconds, or until smooth, then add the crushed ice. Blend again for another 20 seconds, then pour into a tall glass and serve with a stirrer and decorate with the reserved strawberry.

Many of the strawberry liqueurs (crèmes de fraises) contain not only the everyday varieties of strawberries that we are all familiar with, but also the very delicate wild strawberry. Made in countries as diverse as France and Australia, this modern liqueur is becoming very popular.

ALTERNATIVE For a richer cocktail, add ½ measure heavy cream in addition to the cream of coconut.

Mandarin Highball

SERVES 1

Ingredients

crushed ice
5 measures Mandarine Napoléon
2 measures mandarin juice
dash Angostura bitters
8 measures bitter lemon
lemon slice, to decorate

Method

Fill a tall glass halfway with crushed ice, then pour over the Mandarine Napoléon, mandarin juice, and a dash of Angostura bitters. Stir, then pour in the bitter lemon, decorate with a slice of lemon, and serve with a stirrer.

Highballs became popular in the United States, especially New York, at the end of the nineteenth century. It is a long drink, speedily prepared by simply pouring the ingredients over crushed ice into tall glasses.

ALTERNATIVE For a less alcoholic version, replace the Mandarine Napoléon with orange juice and add 2–3 extra dashes Angostura bitters.

Cups & Punches

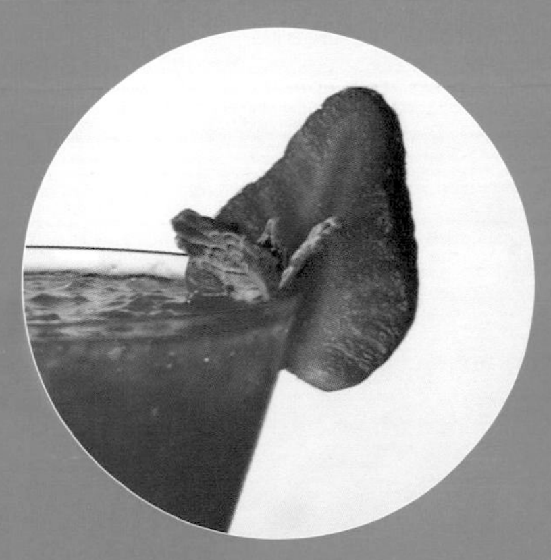

Classic Pimm's

SERVES 8–10

Ingredients

1¼ cups Pimm's No. 1
3 cups lemon-flavor soda
10–12 ice cubes
small piece cucumber, thinly sliced
½ orange, thinly sliced and each slice cut in half
½ red or green apple, cored and sliced
6 strawberries, lightly rinsed, and sliced if large
2–3 borage or mint sprigs

In England, the country where it was invented, this is one of the most popular punches. Invented in 1823 by James Pimm, a farmer's son from Kent who owned an oyster bar in the City of London, Pimm's No. 1 Cup is gin-based and, although its recipe is a closely guarded secret, it is possible to detect subtle aromas of spices and citrus fruits. Since the brand began, there have been five other Pimm's available, with the main difference being the base of alcohol used—recently, the brandy-based Pimm's No. 3 has been reinvented as the seasonal Pimm's Winter—but the No. 1 Cup is the only one that endures and remains a classic drink at summer events.

Variations exist on the classic combination, especially where ingredients might not be available; often, more cucumber replaces the borage leaves and it is even possible to achieve an approximation of Pimm's itself by mixing 1 part gin with 1 part red vermouth and ½ part triple sec or orange curaçao.

Method

Pour the Pimm's and lemon-flavor soda into a large glass serving pitcher and add the ice cubes, cucumber, and prepared fruits. Stir well before adding the borage or mint sprigs. Let stand for flavors to infuse for at least 10 minutes, then serve in tall glasses with spoons.

ALTERNATIVE If you want to serve a single glass of Pimm's, use 1 measure Pimm's to 1 measure lemon-flavor soda or club soda. Use as much or as little fruit as preferred.

Wassail Bowl

SERVES 12

Ingredients

6–8 apples
10 cups ale
⅓ cup sugar
6 measures sweet sherry
1 tsp. freshly grated nutmeg
2-inch piece fresh ginger, grated

Method

Core the apples and place on a baking sheet. Cook in a preheated oven at 400°F for 35–40 minutes until soft. Remove and keep warm. Pour the ale into a saucepan and stir in the sugar and the sherry. Sprinkle in the nutmeg and add the ginger. Heat, stirring, until the sugar has dissolved. Place the apples in individual cups and pour over the hot ale. Serve while still hot with spoons so you can eat the apple.

This is one of the very first "punches" to have been recorded and dates back to the fifteenth century. The original recipe consisted of just three ingredients—ale, brandy, and a little spice. Time, however, has moved on and now there are many variations, most of which produce a far more alcoholic beverage.

ALTERNATIVE For a real traditional flavor, replace the ale with mead.

Champagne Punch

SERVES 14

Ingredients

¾ cup superfine sugar
3 measures brandy
3 measures triple sec
2 measures maraschino syrup from a jar of cherries
1 bottle freshly opened chilled Champagne
1⅓ cups chilled sparkling water
10–12 small ice cubes, to serve
1 cup mixed berries, such as raspberries, strawberries, and blueberries, lightly rinsed, and sliced if large, to serve

You may wonder which glass to use when serving a Champagne Punch—should it be a flute or a coupe or a punch glass? The type of glass has often been dictated by fashion, but really it should be whichever makes the drink taste the best. For a punch, because the Champagne is mixed with other ingredients, a punch glass or coupe glass (*see* page 30) seems best.

Method

Spoon the sugar into a large bowl or punch bowl and pour in the brandy and triple sec. Stir until the sugar has completely dissolved, then stir in the maraschino syrup. Add the Champagne with the sparkling water and the ice cubes, stir, then ladle into champagne glasses and serve with the fruits.

ALTERNATIVE Replace the chilled sparkling water with lemon-flavor soda for a sweeter punch. Cava or sparkling wine could be used in place of the Champagne; try pink sparkling wine.

Boston Punch

SERVES 12–14

Ingredients

1 tbsp. sugar
5½ measures brandy
3 measures triple sec
3 measures dark rum
4 measures freshly squeezed lemon juice
1¼ cups dry hard cider
1 bottle freshly opened chilled Champagne
1¾ cups sparkling water
thin slices red and green apple, to decorate

Method

Sprinkle the sugar into a punch bowl and pour in the brandy. Stir until the sugar has dissolved, then stir in the triple sec, rum, and the lemon juice. Slowly stir in the cider and then the Champagne and water. Add the apple and serve, ensuring that everyone gets 1–2 slices of apple.

It is well worth investing in a punch bowl complete with the glasses and ladle if you frequently have parties. Just the look of the bowl will lift any table and reflect a real party atmosphere.

ALTERNATIVE For a real apple flavor, make as above but replace the hard cider with apple cider and use Calvados. For an added kick, replace the sparkling water with sparkling wine and dilute with club soda.

El Grito

SERVES 8

Ingredients

12 oz. fresh, ripe strawberries
2 tbsp. honey
3 cups (1 bottle) tequila
8–10 ice cubes, crushed

Method

Reserve a few strawberries for decoration, then hull and lightly rinse the remainder. Place in a food processor and add the honey. Blend for 2 minutes, or until a puree is formed. Scrape into a bowl and chill until required. Pour the tequila into a punch bowl and stir in the strawberry puree. Add sufficient crushed ice to create a "slushy" texture. Ladle into glasses and decorate with fresh strawberries.

Every year on September 16, there is much rejoicing as all Mexicans celebrate El Grito. This is when they celebrate Mexico's independence from Spanish rule. So raise a glass and join in the festivities.

ALTERNATIVE Use sugar syrup in place of the honey. Add to taste.

Sangria

SERVES 12

Ingredients

½ apple, cored and sliced
½ orange, cut into small wedges
½ lemon, cut into small slices
6 strawberries, sliced
3¼ cups (1 bottle) Spanish red wine, such as Rioja
4 measures Spanish brandy
1 large orange
1 large, ripe lemon
8 measures club soda or lemon-flavor soda
8 ice cubes, crushed

Method

Place the chopped up fruit in a large serving pitcher or punch bowl and pour in the red wine. Stir in the brandy. Squeeze the juice from the orange and lemon and stir into the wine and brandy together with the club soda or lemon-flavor soda. Add the ice, serve with a straw, if liked, and a large spoon to enable stirring and the fruit to be placed into the glasses.

There can be nothing better than sitting in the hot sun on a Spanish terrace or beach, sipping a glass or two of Sangria while watching the world go by. It even works at home, as long as the weather is hot and sunny.

ALTERNATIVE Try using rosé wine in place of the red wine and a little honey, if a sweeter drink is preferred.

Rosy Punch

SERVES 14–16

Ingredients

6½ cups (2 bottles) chilled rosé wine
6 measures brandy
6 measures raspberry syrup
1½ cups tonic water
1 lemon, preferably organic, thinly sliced and cut into half moons
10 ice cubes

Method

Pour the rosé wine into a punch bowl and stir in the brandy and raspberry syrup. Stir well, then add the tonic water, the lemon slices, and ice cubes.

Rosé or blush wines are sometimes referred to as summertime wines, but are rapidly growing in popularity the whole year round. They are produced in France, Italy, Spain, and Portugal, as well as the New World countries, and there is bound to be a wine to suit every taste.

ALTERNATIVE If liked, make your own raspberry syrup. Lightly rinse 2½ cups fresh or frozen raspberries, place in a heavy saucepan, and add ¼ cup sugar and 2 tablespoons water. Place over gentle heat and cook for 10 minutes, or until the fruit has collapsed. Cool, then pass through a food processor and rub through a strainer to remove any seeds. Store in a screw-top jar in the refrigerator for up to 1 week.

Creole Punch

SERVES 10–12

When making a punch to serve, it is always a good idea to have some extra "mixers," such as soda or tonic water, to add to the punch in case it is too strong.

Ingredients

12 ice cubes, crushed
1 bottle port
6 measures, or to taste, brandy
3 measures freshly squeezed lemon juice
lemon-flavor soda
orange and lemon half-moons and kiwi slices, to decorate

Method

Place the crushed ice in a punch bowl and pour over the port and brandy. Add the lemon juice, then stir well. Pour into glasses and top off with the soda. Spear the orange, lemon, and kiwi slices onto a toothpick, then arrange on the glass and serve with a stirrer and a straw.

ALTERNATIVE Make a single glass using the same method and using the following amounts: 4 ice cubes, crushed; 2 measures port; ½ measure brandy; and 2 teaspoons freshly squeezed lemon juice. Decorate as above.

Knockout Punch

SERVES 12

Hard cider is made mainly from specially grown varieties of apple and generally has a strong alcoholic content (over 5 percent), is yellow in color, and often cloudy.

Ingredients

4⅓ cups hard cider
2–3 measures gin
2–3 measures brandy
2 measures peach schnapps, or use extra brandy
2–3 tbsp. honey (optional)
2 ripe peaches, pitted and sliced or chopped
1¼ cups lemon-flavor soda

Method

Pour the cider into a punch bowl and stir in the gin, brandy, and peach schnapps or extra brandy. Add the clear honey to taste and the sliced or chopped peaches. Chill for up to 2 hours. When ready, stir in the lemon-flavor soda, then serve.

ALTERNATIVE You may see some Knockout Punches made with tequila and rum.

Claret Cup

SERVES 8–10

It may seem unusual to use a claret and then to serve it chilled. In fact, if you lived in France, this would not be at all unusual because, in the summer months, red wine is frequently served slightly chilled. It is delicious and perfect for a warm summer evening. Try it and see.

Ingredients

- 4 tbsp. sugar syrup (*see* page 31)
- zest and juice from 1 lemon, preferably organic
- zest and juice from 2 small oranges, preferably organic
- 2 measures brandy
- 1 bottle claret
- 1½ cups tonic water
- 2–3 borage sprigs, if available
- thin slices from ½ orange and ½ lemon

Method

Place the sugar syrup in a heavy saucepan. Add the zest to the sugar syrup and bring to a boil, reduce the heat, and simmer gently for 10 minutes. Remove and let cool, then strain, discarding the peel. Stir the strained syrup and the lemon and orange juices into a punch bowl, then stir in the brandy, claret, and tonic water. Chill for up to 1 hour before decorating with the borage and fruit slices and serving.

ALTERNATIVE Add the tonic (chilled) after the cup has chilled for an hour, if you want to retain its fizziness. The recipe would work well on hot summer evenings if the claret were replaced with a bottle of roséwine.

Honeysuckle Cup

SERVES 12

Ingredients

1 bottle medium-dry white wine, such as a chardonnay
1 tbsp. honey
2 measures brandy
2½ cups lemon-flavor soda
1 ripe peach, pitted, sliced, and chopped
⅓ cup sliced, lightly rinsed strawberries
8 ice cubes, crushed

Method

Pour the wine into a punch bowl and stir in the honey and brandy. Stir until the honey has completely dissolved, then stir in the soda, sliced fruits, and crushed ice. Let stand for 30 minutes before serving.

When choosing wine to use in a cup or punch, it is always a good idea to use a reasonably good wine. Using cheap inferior wine can cost you more money in the end, as you could spend both time and money trying to improve the finished result, and you may end up disappointed.

ALTERNATIVE This makes a perfect drink to enjoy for a summer celebration. To make it even more special, replace the lemon-flavor soda with sparkling wine.

Midsummer Night's Dream

SERVES 16–18

Ingredients

1 bottle white wine, such as Riesling
1 bottle red wine, such as Beaujolais
2 measures Cointreau
2–3 tbsp. honey
1 slice galia melon
1 ripe peach
10 ice cubes, crushed
10 ripe strawberries, halved
2½ cups lemon-flavor soda
few fresh herbs

Method

Pour the wine into a punch bowl and stir in the Cointreau and honey. Stir until the honey has completely dissolved. Discard the skin and seeds from the melon, then dice into small pieces. Lightly rinse the peach, cut in half, and discard the pit. Chop and add to the bowl with the ice, strawberries, soda and herbs. Stir, then let stand for 30 minutes to let the flavors develop, then serve.

This cup is absolutely delightful and the perfect drink to offer in the summer, either during the day or in the evening. Try using borage, if available, or a few mint sprigs, or even a little lemon balm.

ALTERNATIVE Use a variety of different fruits according to availability and preference. Try mixed berries, such as raspberries, blueberries, and strawberries, fresh cherries, or even apples, pears, and fresh blackberries.

Caribbean Toddy

SERVES 2

A "toddy" is normally associated with Scotch whisky, but, in fact, as long as the drink has some liquor, a hint of a citrus fruit, and sweetness, it is entitled to be called a toddy.

Ingredients

5 measures white rum
1 tsp. raw sugar
⅔ cup boiling water
6 drops Angostura bitters
½ tsp. finely grated lime zest
2 lime twists, to decorate
freshly grated nutmeg, to serve

Method

Pour the white rum into a blender or cocktail shaker and add the sugar. Pour over the boiling water and blend or shake until dissolved. Add the Angostura bitters and lime zest and shake again until mixed. Pour into heatproof glasses, add a lime twist to each, sprinkle with a little grated nutmeg, and serve.

ALTERNATIVE For a nonalcoholic version, replace the white rum with freshly brewed, hot black tea.

Glühwein

SERVES 8

Ingredients

2½ cups red wine, such as Burgundy
¼ cup light brown sugar
4 whole cloves
2 cinnamon sticks, lightly bruised
1 tsp. whole allspice
1 lemon, preferably organic, thinly sliced
4 measures brandy

From ancient Rome, where one Gavius Apicius recorded his recipe for Spiced Wine Surprise, using pepper, mace, aromatic leaf, saffron, dates, and roasted date pits, to ancient India, where priests used mulled punch in temple rituals, the history of heating wine and spices goes back centuries. It may have been done in order to revive wine that had gone bad and to sustain health in the winter (it was probably more sanitary than water).

Also known as Mulled Wine or many other names depending on the country you are in, warming and atmospheric Glühwein—as it is known in Germany—is synonymous with "après ski," winter markets and Christmas. It is a perfect drink for any cold evening. Spicing and ingredients also vary greatly—almonds and raisins are often added to Scandinavian Glögg—but the recipe provided here features the classic use of cloves, cinnamon, and allspice; there are also many other hearty, warming winter drinks in this chapter.

Method

Pour the wine into a heavy saucepan and stir in the sugar. Add the cloves, cinnamon sticks, and allspice. Heat gently, stirring frequently, until the sugar has dissolved. Cut the lemon slices into half moons, then add to the saucepan. Heat gently for about 15–20 minutes until the wine is just below boiling point. Add the brandy and heat gently for another 5 minutes. Strain into heatproof glasses and serve.

ALTERNATIVE Wrap the spices in a small piece of cheesecloth instead of just placing them in the wine and sugar. This will make their removal far easier and there is no need to strain.

Christmas Wine

SERVES 12

This is a fantastic drink to enjoy by the fire at Christmas time. The alcohol-soaked raisins take on so much flavor that they add another dimension to the drinking experience.

Ingredients

1½ cups (½ bottle) gin
1 bottle red wine, such as Burgundy
½ cup seedless raisins
¼ cup light brown sugar
6 green cardamom pods, lightly cracked
3 whole cloves
1 cinnamon stick, lightly bruised
thinly pared zest from ½ lemon

Method

Pour the gin and red wine into a heavy saucepan and add the raisins and sugar. Tie the spices and lemon zest into a small square of cheesecloth and add to the saucepan. Heat gently, stirring frequently, for 12–15 minutes, then bring to just below boiling point. Stir occasionally. Remove the cloth bag of spices, then ladle into heatproof glasses and serve.

ALTERNATIVE If gin is not your drink, replace with either brandy or whiskey—both work really well and are guaranteed to get everyone in the Christmas mood.

Hot Spicy Cider

SERVES 8

Ingredients

5 cups dry hard cider
¼–⅓ cup, or to taste, sugar
6 whole cloves
2 cinnamon sticks, lightly bruised
3 whole star anise
1 small orange, thinly sliced and cut into half moons

Method

Pour the cider into a heavy saucepan and place over medium heat. Add the sugar together with the whole cloves, cinnamon sticks, and the star anise. Add the orange half moons to the saucepan, then heat gently, stirring frequently, until the sugar has completely dissolved. Strain into heatproof glasses and serve with 1–2 half-moon orange slices.

In order to get the maximum flavor from the cinnamon sticks, it is important that they are lightly bruised. Simply wrap in a piece of plastic wrap or paper towels and smash lightly with a rolling pin or meat mallet. Use as directed.

ALTERNATIVE Add a touch of the exotic and add to the spices used above with 4 cracked cardamom pods, 2 lightly bruised lemongrass stalks, and 1 small piece fresh ginger, lightly smashed, along with with the star anise and whole cloves.

Funchal Cup

SERVES 18–20

Ingredients

1 bottle Madeira
2 measures brandy
4 measures apricot brandy
4 measures kirsch
2½ cups freshly squeezed orange juice
1 cinnamon stick, lightly bruised
1¼ cups water
¼ cup, or to taste, light brown sugar

Funchal is the capital city of Portugal's Madeira islands and hence lends its name to this delicious winter warmer using the fortified wine Madeira. Madeira was originally an unfortified ordinary red wine and, when it became popular with American colonialists, they began taking it over to the New World. However, the long journey in casks aboard ship proved to have a fortuitous effect: the heat and exposure to oxygen, causing oxidization, led to a fine-tasting fortified wine with impressive durability. From then on, its popularity soared and it began to be produced commercially, using a process called "estufagem," in which the wine is heated to recreate the effects of the long, hot journey.

The success of Madeira peaked in the nineteenth century with many British merchants entering the wine trade. By the end of the century, however, two diseases—Oidium and Phylloxera—decimated crops and all but ruined the industry. Today, however, Madeira enjoys recovered popularity, along with other rich wines, as ideal to drink with meals—and, of course, divine in concoctions such as the Funchal Cup!

Method

Pour the Madeira and both brandies into a heavy saucepan and add the kirsch together with the orange juice and cinnamon stick. Stir in the water and sugar, then place over gentle heat. Bring slowly to just below boiling point, stirring frequently, until the sugar has completely dissolved. Check for sweetness (adding more sugar, if preferred) and for the alcoholic strength. Add more water, if liked, and heat gently until hot. Serve in heatproof glasses.

ALTERNATIVE Serve with a long cinnamon stick to use as a stirrer, or omit some of the sugar and serve with a sugar swizzle stick.

Mulled Ale

SERVES 8–10

Ingredients

1 lemon, preferably organic
½ tsp. freshly grated nutmeg
¼ tsp. ground cinnamon
2 tbsp. raw sugar
1¼ cups water
2½ cups ale
3 measures brandy
1 measure rum
1 measure gin

Method

Thinly pare the zest from the lemon and place in a heavy saucepan. Sprinkle in the freshly grated nutmeg and cinnamon, then stir in the sugar and water. Squeeze out the juice from the lemon and strain into the saucepan. Place over gentle heat and bring to a boil, stirring. When the sugar has dissolved, stir in the ale, brandy, rum, and gin. Heat gently for 12–15 minutes until hot but not boiling. Ladle into heatproof glasses and serve.

In the fifteenth and sixteenth centuries, ale was the common drink, as water was far too toxic. Tea and coffee were almost unheard of, as were fruit juices, so ale and wine were commonplace. To make ale more palatable for some, spices were added that greatly enhanced the flavor, especially when served warm. The recipe here is a modern version of the idea of spicing up ale.

ALTERNATIVE Try using hard cider in place of the ale and add a sliced apple to the bowl before heating.

The Bishop

SERVES 12–14

Ingredients

12 whole cloves
1 lemon, preferably organic
1½ bottles ruby port
2½ cups water
¼ cup sugar
1 tsp. ground allspice
cinnamon sticks, for stirring

Method

Preheat the oven to 350°F. Stick the whole cloves into the lemon, then roast in the oven for 30 minutes. Remove and place in a heatproof bowl. Pour in the port with the water and sugar and sprinkle in the allspice. Place over a saucepan of gently simmering water and heat for 30 minutes, or until very hot. Serve hot with cinnamon stick stirrers.

This traditional recipe is often served around Christmas time. The nineteenth-century cookbook writer Eliza Acton has been credited with the development of this punch and Charles Dickens also mentions it in some of his novels. It can also be called The Smoking Bishop.

ALTERNATIVE Try roasting an orange instead of a lemon.

Bahamas Punch

SERVES 12

Ingredients

½ cup, or to taste, light brown sugar
1¼ cups water
1 lemon, preferably organic
3 small oranges, preferably organic
1¼ cups cold, strong black tea
3 cups (1 bottle) dark rum
fresh pineapple wedges and orange spirals, to decorate

Method

Place the sugar into a heavy saucepan and pour in the water. Thinly pare the zest from the lemon and 1 of the oranges and add to the saucepan. Heat gently, stirring frequently, for 12–15 minutes until the sugar has dissolved. Bring to a boil and boil for 5 minutes, then remove from the heat. Squeeze out the juice from all the fruits and add to the saucepan together with the tea and rum. Stir, then strain into heatproof glasses, decorate, and serve.

Rum is made from distilling fermented sugar and water. The sugar comes from sugar cane and is fermented from cane juice. Concentrated cane juice or molasses is the sweet, sticky residue that remains after the sugar has been extracted and the juice boiled off. The molasses is used with minerals and other trace elements to make rum.

ALTERNATIVE Use white rum in place of the dark rum and add a little fresh pineapple to the bowl before heating.

Summer Cup

SERVES 12–14

Ingredients

1 bottle sparkling white wine
3 measures white rum
2 measures freshly squeezed orange juice
3 measures freshly squeezed lemon juice
4 measures pineapple juice
2 tbsp., or to taste, honey
8 ice cubes, crushed
1¼ cups ginger ale
¼ cup fresh raspberries, 1 peach, and 2–3 mint sprigs, to decorate

Method

Pour the sparkling wine into a punch bowl and stir in the rum with the strained fruit juices. Add the honey and stir until dissolved, then add the crushed ice and the ginger ale. Lightly rinse the raspberries, slice the peach, and cut into small pieces. Add to the punch together with the mint sprigs and serve.

When using honey, it is not always easy to measure accurately. There are two good ways that work every time. Heat a measuring spoon in very hot water, dip into the honey, and scoop out the amount; or heat the jar for 30 seconds in the microwave, then measure.

ALTERNATIVE For a fruity cup, replace the ginger ale with the same amount of freshly brewed fruit tea, let cool, then add to the bowl.

Apple Cider Cup

SERVES 12

When using the zest from citrus fruits, it is always a good idea to scrub thoroughly. This will remove any wax, pesticides, or fertilizers that may be present.

Ingredients

2 apples
1 lemon, preferably organic
8 whole cloves
4 tbsp. sugar syrup
(*see* page 31)
6½ cups hard cider
1¼ cups club soda

Method

Cut the apples into quarters and core, then slice thinly and place in a heatproof bowl. Thinly pare the zest from the lemon and add to the bowl together with the strained juice from the lemon. Add the whole cloves. Heat the sugar syrup to just below boiling point, then pour over the apples. Let cool. Carefully pour in the cider together with the club soda and serve.

ALTERNATIVE Serve with ice, if liked.

Tropical Cup

SERVES 16

Ingredients

1¼ cups dark rum
1 cup apricot brandy
1¼ cups pineapple juice
1¼ cups freshly squeezed pink grapefruit juice
6 measures freshly squeezed orange juice
8 measures mango juice
3 ripe passion fruits
10 ice cubes, crushed
1 small, ripe mango and 16 maraschino cherries, to decorate

Method

Pour the rum and brandy into a punch bowl and stir in all the fruit juices. Scoop out the flesh, seeds, and juice from the passion fruits and stir into the bowl together with the crushed ice. Peel and pit the mango, then cut into small dice and stir into the punch together with the maraschino cherries. Serve.

The Caribbean is the home of rum, and every island produces their own brand. Rum is also produced in Barbados, Cuba, the Dominican Republic, Guyana, Haiti, Jamaica, and Martinique, all creating their own special, closely guarded recipe.

ALTERNATIVE Add more tropical fruits to the cup. Try chopped papaya, pineapple, and mango. Do not throw the fruit away; serve with ice cream as a luscious dessert.

Dr. Johnson's Choice

SERVES 10–12

It is widely believed that this punch was the favorite tipple of, and was named after, Dr. Samuel Johnson, who was responsible for his "Dictionary of the English Language."

Ingredients

3¼ cups (1 bottle) red wine, such as a Merlot
12 sugar lumps
6 whole cloves
2½ cups boiling water
4 measures curaçao
4 measures brandy
freshly grated nutmeg

Method

Pour the wine into a heavy saucepan and add the sugar lumps and whole cloves. Place over gentle heat and bring to just below boiling point. Add the boiling water together with the curaçao and brandy. Pour into heatproof glasses and serve with a little freshly grated nutmeg on top.

ALTERNATIVE Add 2–4 cinnamon sticks to the wine when heating and serve with extra cinnamon sticks to stir.

Bacardi & Champagne Punch

SERVES 16

Ingredients

8 measures white Bacardi rum
5 measures triple sec
5 measures amaretto liqueur
2 measures grenadine
3 measures sugar syrup (*see* page 31)
1 small pineapple
3¼ cups (1 bottle) Champagne, chilled
2½ cups sparkling water, chilled

Method

Pour the Bacardi white rum into a punch bowl and stir in the triple sec, amaretto liqueur, grenadine, and sugar syrup. Stir. Discard the plume, skin, and hard central core from the pineapple and cut the fruit into small wedges. Add to the punch bowl, cover lightly, and chill for at least 2 hours. When ready to serve, stir in the chilled Champagne and the sparkling water and serve.

It was in the early nineteenth century that Don Facundo Bacardi Masso, a winemaker, attempted to "tame" rum. He made several attempts to refine the flavor and finally filtered the alcohol through charcoal, which removed many of the impurities. By aging the rum in oak barrels, it mellowed to become "white" or clear rum, which now constitutes what we know as Bacardi rum.

ALTERNATIVE To lessen the alcoholic impact of this drink, try substituting the triple sec or liqueur with apricot or guava nectar.

Index